Bread in a Starving Africa

Murv L. Kandakai Gardiner, PhD

authorHOUSE®

AuthorHouse™
1663 Liberty Drive
Bloomington, IN 47403
www.authorhouse.com
Phone: 833-262-8899

Published by AuthorHouse 03/21/2023

ISBN: 979-8-8230-0101-4 (sc)
ISBN: 979-8-8230-0102-1 (e)

Print information available on the last page.

Contents

Dedication

I dedicate this book to my mother Lucinda Isabel Gardiner, grandmothers Danielette Francis Gardiner and Carolyn Hutchins Ferguson, my father Theodore M. Gardiner, grandfathers Theophilus Momolu Gardiner and Henry JR Cooper, my sisters TD, Lottie Gardiner Harmon, Danielette (Tayty) Gardiner Kiadii, Morrie Wokie Gardiner, brothers Tilmon Momolu Gardiner, Theodore (Dara) Gardiner, Jr., Francis Robert Gardiner, Christian Allison, and Henry (Sir. Patrick) Gardiner, cousins Leonard Theophilus Deshield, McKinley Alfred Deshield, Jr, and Frances Deshield Freeman.

Introduction

Africa our native land has bread in its starving land. Africa the motherland gave birth to the first human hand. Africa my fatherland came into being by God's Holy hand. Africa a promised land must become a place where all her children can play peacefully in the sand. Africa another Jerusalem, cries for her children to stop shedding blood upon her sacred land.

In this corpus of ideas, I shall present Liberia, the land of my birth as a prototype of starving lands in order to understand the lingering problem of poverty in Africa. In so doing, we shall be employing some interdisciplinary tools to bring to consciousness, intellectual and spiritual bread in a starving Africa.

I am writing because I would like for so many people in Liberia who are starving to find bread. I feel impelled to write this treatise because unlike millions of children in Africa, I was blessed with two loving parents, Theodore and Lucinda Gardiner who in addition to providing me, my siblings, and cousins with physical bread in a starving land, were able to raise us in the environment of spiritual bread. They taught us in our formative stages, the words of Jesus, "I am the bread of life. He that cometh to me shall never hunger." (KJV John 6:35) Additionally, as my uncle James and aunt Florence Cooper prepared hot organic bread and margarine butter for me and my cousins Matthew, Fritz, and Harrington, they explicated to us the significance of Jesus' miracle at the wedding in Cana of Galilee. And as I looked forward to my grandmother Caroline's Palm Butter, I always knew that I would also be given spiritual sustenance at Revivals with her. Also, my aunt Annie Marquis baked bread on several occasions in Georgia and sent them to me during my studies at Princeton Theological Seminary via Trailways Bus Services.

"Where can I find bread?" This has always been the cry of starving children, families, and communities devastated by famines and wars. But one does not have to wait to see such devastation on an American television or internet. As soon as we leave America and get back home to Africa, we find the problem ubiquitous with children, women, and men understandingly begging for their daily bread. Thus, the cry of the poor, the cry for bread is God's own cry as well. Today the cry for bread in Liberia is attributable to the perennial and deadly conflicts in battles being waged by *thanatos* against *eros,* the death instincts against the life instincts of some Liberians as Sigmund Freud posits, and by "the devil himself who prevents and hinders the stability of all government and honorable, peaceable relations on earth," as Martin Luther puts it.[1]

So where can one find bread? The answer begins with the definition of bread in its specific African context and larger global context. In Africa and in Palestine, bread obviously was made from barley wheat. In Ethiopia, Eritrea, and Liberia bread is the essential element of basic diet. While many Ethiopians make the distinction between *dabbo* (Western & Mediterranean semblances of bread) from *injera* (organic grain from Teff seed flour), and

---

[1] Martin Luther, *Exposition on the Lord's Prayer*

Liberians show a sharp difference between American wheat or corn bread from *fu-fu* and soup, they share a commonality with some sub-cultures of the world that consider bread/dough as money. "All bread is God-given, sent down from heaven giving life to the world,"[2] as Weatherhead avers. All the prophets of the Eastern world including Noah, Abraham, Moses, Isaiah, Jeremiah, Mohammed, the apostles, and St Augustine posited that without God's gifts of rain and grain, there would be no cornfields and consequently, no bread.

Bread means food but it also entails every meaningful expression that proceeds from the mouth of God. Throughout this meditative corpus, I shall primarily speak of bread in the Aramaic connotation of bread (*lachma*) because it is within the Hebrew family of wisdom (*hochma*). And as Hegel defines **mind** as love[3], I would also argue that bread is love and love is bread, as love is the greatest expression from God to his creation, and because the one whose name is love, who came down from heaven to be the bread of life, historically was born in *Bethlehem* (house of bread). Bread/love then becomes a positive attitude toward life as it both symbolizes humanity's dependence upon God and our responsibility toward this sacred earth. As St Augustine and others have accentuated, Without God we cannot make a loaf. And without us God will not make a loaf. One day in Palestine after a long day of teaching, healing, and other acts of caring, looking at the multitude of people in his midst, Jesus asked his disciple Philip,

---

[2] Leslie Weatherhead, *The Autobiography of Jesus, meaning, what Jesus said about himself*

[3] Georg Hegel, *The Phenomenology of Mind*

Where can we buy bread that these may eat? Philip answered, two hundred denari of bread is not sufficient for them. One of his disciples, Andrew, Simon Peter's brother saith to him, "There is a boy, who has five barley loaves, and two small fishes; but what are these among so many?" And Jesus said, "make the men sit down. The men sat down in number about five thousand. And Jesus took the loaves, and having given thanks, distributed them to the disciples, and to those who had sat down likewise the fishes, as much as they wished. And after they were satisfied, he said to his disciples, Gather the fragments which are left that nothing may be lost." (KJV John 6: 6-13)

Jesus spoke and five loaves of bread were transformed and became five thousand. First, he spoke in words of thanks to God. Then he spoke deeply from his heart in feeling the hunger and thirst of the multitude. He intended for the bread distributed to his disciples to grow in their hands. Ultimately, after raising his eyes to heaven, he broke the loaves and allocated them to his disciples. The above passage and the synoptic Mark, Matthew, and Luke Gospels teach us that all bread must be broken before its spiritual and physical ingredients can be imparted into a suffering and dying humanity. Anthropology reminds us that the first form of communication by humans and primates was breaking bread. Every worldview posits some significance on breaking bread appertaining to divine and human fellowship. Yet some men and women in Liberia have disrespected their maker by fighting each other, in some cases, right after they ate before their God.

Carl Jung's theory of the *Collective Unconscious* accentuates that hostility and civility, fear and faith have all originated from our animal and human ancestors and filtered through to us. Moreover, for this writer, metaphorically, there is a spiritual DNA/Nature (God, the earth, & our ancestors) and a spiritual Nurture/Environment (God, heaven, our parents, & institutions of redemption). Thus, in both the spiritual nature and nurture above mentioned, children of Liberia and the rest of Africa can find the needed bread instead of "rebel" armies that feed the greed and omnipotence of some would be political leaders. We are called by our own African heritage and God our maker to cast our lot with whom Frantz Fanon calls "the Wretched of the Earth"[4] and to be ecologically responsible for this sacred earth. The Gospels instruct us that God blesses and increases our enterprises when we seek to further the welfare of others.

I can never forget my late aunts Danielette G. DosSantos, Cecelia Gardiner, and uncle Jean DosSantos, who picked me up that early winter morning in that frigid degree and shortly after fed me daily with bread, love, and support. A word of thanks goes to my three girls Shelise, Sherisse, and Pen. I also thank Ken and Linda Maccari who always provided me with distinctive bread of *paraklesis*. A word of thanks goes to Doc and Mulu Ababa who gaved me Kit'ta, unleavened bread in Addis, to the kerygma group at Trinity/St. Philip Episcopal Cathedral, Trinity and Northeastern Presbyterian Churches, to Reid Memorial, Zion Hill and Bethesda Presbyterian Churches, North Wilkesboro and Beulah Presbyterian Churches, St. Mark & St. Matthias Episcopal Churches, the Tuesday Bible Study & Brotherhood Fellowship at St Edwards Episcopal Church. A further word of thankfulness goes to teachers Hannah Bush, Lita Anderson, Telyta Cooper, cousins Melita Cummings, Lucinda Anderson,

---

[4] See Fanon's *The Wretched of the Earth*, (New York, 1961)

Evita Cooper, Rev Anne Cooper, Eugenia Gardiner, Louis Fredericks, Grace Dennis, Louis Dennis, aunts Beatrice Wilson, Bernice Cooper, Betty Brewer, Gurley Toles, Annie Brent, Ma Josephine Barnes, Ma Clyde Harmon, Ma Annie Hamilton, Ma Ella Scott, Ma Nedly, aunt Melita Gardiner, my uncle Dr. James Marquis a major source of inspiration, my Godmother Gertrude, God-sisters Joyce and Ora, sister-in law Florence Tolbert Gardiner who fed us with *Split Peas and Rice,* sister-in law Marian Gardiner for providing spiritual nourishment, sister-in law Ruby Johnson G, sister-in law Hannah Saba Gardiner-Thomas who in her authenticity has always provided intellectual bread, sister-in law Davidetta and Rachel with IT, sisters-in-law Pauline and Roberta in providing sustenance of *Short Bread,* my sisters Theo, Annie, Lucinda, and Vero for all their love and support, my brothers Harrington and Richlieu, nieces Ebony Cummings and Fiona Williams for their tremendous assistance, other nieces, nephews, and cousins. Words are inadequate to express the depth of thankfulness to Kathy Sulkes and Janice Headley of the MacMillan Center for International Studies at Yale University. Both Kathy and Janice provided daily sustenance of Mediterranean bread and roasted lamb to all of us during Yale's extensive International Institutes from Summer 2003 – 2006, They also facilitated scholarships for me to be fed with the bread of knowledge from experts like Professors Brachen, Geddes, Kennedy, and others at Luce Hall. Professors Clark Moustakas of Union Institute & University, James Patrick Kelley, William Peck and Peter Kaufmann of UNC Chapel Hill, Donald Capps, Charles West, Freda Gardiner, and J. Christian Beker at Princeton Theological Seminary, Gayle Tate and Leonard Bethel of Rutgers University were all major contexts of intellectual bread for me.

Because I've been blessed, I close my Introduction with thanks to my late aunt Rachel Gardiner who fed us daily when we were children with this prayer:

> Almighty and everlasting God, in whom we live and move and have our being; We, thy needed creatures, render thee our humble praises, for thy preservation of us from the beginning of our lives to this day, and especially for having delivered us from the dangers of the past night. For these thy mercies, we bless and magnify thy glorious name; humbly beseeching thee to accept this our morning sacrifice of praise and thanksgiving; for his sake who lay down in the grave, and rose again for us, thy Son our Savior Jesus Christ. Amen.[5]

And from Daniel Coker: We have anchored about thirty miles from Sherbro Island. The sand has a handsome appearance, looks level. We have to labor between hope and fear as to our reception. Oh, God! Is there not for us a place wherein to rest the soles of our feet? Will not Africa open her bosom, and receive her weeping and bleeding children that may be taken from slave ships or come from America?

When will Jehovah hear our cries?
When will the sun of freedom rise?
When will for us a Moses stand,
And bring us out from Pharaoh's hand?

Murv L. Kandakai Gardiner, Ph.D.
Sidist Kilo, Addis Ababa, Ethiopia and Cape Palmas, Liberia

---

[5] My auntie's prayer was taken from *The 1928 Book of Common Prayer* and Coker's prayer, taken from *Prayer at Sea*, Saturday, March 18, 1820

1

The Loaf

We begin this corpus with the symbol of wholeness. The loaf is a symbol of wholeness. And this wholeness is what some men and women psychologically, economically, and spiritually strive for. In their psychological orientations Carl Jung, Abraham Maslow, and Carl Rogers contributed some insights on how one attains completeness. For Jung, it is finding a balance between the *anima* and *animus*. It is also the complete integration of the *persona* and *shadow* and *anima* and *animus*. Jung's theory of wholeness elucidates the inner dynamic of human development. Unlike Freud, Jung stipulates that the unconscious is positive with the hidden, inner self having a proclivity for God. However, the interplay of the *persona* and *shadow* does impact one's striving for integration and wholeness. For Maslow, one achieves wholeness via the fulfillment of self-actualization and self-transcendence. And for Rogers, it is having congruence, unconditional positive regard, and empathic resonance. We indeed find tremendous utility in all three theoretical foundations as we seek to either avert being broken or gain restoration to wholeness. However, the loaf is a symbol of our true dependence on God and not an idolatrous dependence on political, cultural, and individual traditions and institutions. Mark, the Gospel writer, in the following passage illustrates this point:

> The disciples had forgotten to bring bread except for one loaf they had with them in the boat. "Be careful," Jesus warned them. "Watch out for the leaven of the Pharisees and the leaven of Herod." They discussed this with one another and said, "it is because we have no bread." Aware of their discussion, Jesus asked them, why are you talking about having no bread? Do you still not see or understand? Are your hearts hardened? You have eyes but fail to see, and ears but fail to hear? And do you not remember? When I broke the five loaves for the five thousand, how many baskets full of pieces did you pick up?" "Twelve," they replied. "And when I broke the seven loaves for the four thousand, how many basket-full of pieces did you pick up?" They answered, "seven." He said to them, "Do you still not understand?" (ESV Mark 8:14-21)

Is it ironic that the one loaf the disciples happened to bring with them in the boat symbolizes Jesus the *Loaf,* the totality/wholeness of life that will be broken to make men and women whole? Calvin calls the disciples' negative cognitive habits here "**shameful ingratitude,** because after witnessing the power of God as bread was created out of nothing twice, they were anxious about bread as if the Master did not possess the same power."[6]

In Christian faith we must never be satisfied with the world as it is (Moltmann, 1979). Accordingly, we must never be complacent regarding the leavens of the Herodians of this world. Leaven is hypocrisy. It is the

---

[6] Jean Calvin, *Harmony of the Evangelists: Matthew, Mark, & Luke*

direct antithesis of the Hebrew *emet* and the Amharic *onet* (the truth) of God. Thus, contextually, leaven is false doctrine. True believers can diligently be watchful by keeping a perpetual Passover with unleavened bread because God knows the hearts and sees the depths of all men and women. In their lingering struggle for omnipotence (vain glory and power), some men and women in Liberia wear the masks of religion, even in their continuous sycophancy to their idols of oppression while attempting to impose their will upon God just to further their exploitative politics instead of submitting to the glory of God. We were blessed to have an economist and a vibrant president despite some misgiving in the personage of Ellen Johnson Sirleaf who committed herself to working with Africa and the world via a variety of initiatives to significantly alleviate infant mortality, poverty, and gender asymmetry.

Jesus' questions in antiquity, "Do you have eyes but fail to see, and ears but fail to hear...do you not remember, and do you not understand?" are pivotal for Liberia. This leaven/evil that was against a compassionate and inclusive government (EJS'), was repetitive and cyclical because the yeasts of Satan puffed some people up. As Jean Calvin critically observes, when surrounded by an environment of evil, the human mind has a natural proclivity toward vanity. As my dad use to teach me in the words of the psalmist,

> "Unless the Lord builds the city, they labor in vain that build it." (Psalm 127)

Here even the anointed King of Israel does affirm that it is God and God alone who governs the home, economic, and political affairs of men and women. Even though some of us tendentiously rob God of the honor due to his holy name by behaving as if we have made all accomplishments by ourselves, we can never gain anything in permanence without the providence of God. And as Calvin in his *Harmony* passionately directs us to **Jesus** the **Loaf** as he asserts, "Unless God feeds us daily, the largest accumulation of the necessaries of life will be of no avail, we shall famish in the midst of plenty unless what we are watered by, is the secret blessings of God."[7] Thus, any accumulation of wealth by anybody, at any place, and at any time at the expense of the massive poor shall perish. In view of the above, Calvin adds, "Every man must submit to the toil of his calling."[8] That is why my late grandfather Theophilus Momolu Gardiner, Sr, Suffragan Bishop of the Episcopal Church, provided sustenance in addition to grain and other modes of bread to many Liberians. And that is why Leymah Gbowee challenged the dehumanization of many women amidst the brutality of the Liberian Civil War and the continuous marginalization of women and children during an unregenerate political dispensation by calling upon the Power of God.

In order to have a qualitative future in Liberia, parents and children must pray daily for strength to spiritually defeat the tyrannical rapacity of Satan that is embodied in the idols of war. Christ never held a sword in his hand. But when he spoke, the powers of Satan were destroyed in such a spiritual immediacy, that Lazarus, Jairus' daughter, and the woman with menorrhagia, who in hemorrhaging met what the *DSM-IV* calls undifferentiated somatoform disorder in its ACD&E criteria, were

---

[7] *Harmony of the Evangelists, Mark, Matthew, & Luke*

[8] Ibid

healed. And two paralytic men (Mark 2: 9 – 12 and John 5: 6 – 9) were healed. These paralytics were thought to have suffered from conversion disorder. Their disease was also attributable to genetic flat-footedness and/ or *intermittent claudicating* – *Claudication* (Jean-Martin Charcot) and *Oedipus* (Freud) which also means swollen foot. Yet despite their very deep psychological conflicts/anxieties which led to the symbolic resolution of the problem, which was conversion disorder, Jesus employed a directive method/command for them to stand up, pick up their mats and begin walking. They obeyed and were healed. In the Mark's account, though the man was healed vicariously, according to Jesus, because of the faith of his four friends, the people who witnessed this therapeutic intervention were amazed, and they all glorified God, saying, "We have never seen anything like this!" (NIV Mark 2:12) So who are we to succumb to the Anti-Christ in our own age as he is manufacturing some would be leaders in Liberia irrespective of ethnicity for further oppression?

Mark, the Gospel writer, uses the symbol of the loaf to drive home three points of engagement of reconciliation that Jesus employs with his disciples. The first point is a word of caution. "Take heed, beware of the leaven of the Pharisees and the leaven of Herod!" (KJV Mark 8:15) Be aware of the hardening of hearts which is the Pharisees' lack of faith and understanding. For Matthew, another Gospel writer, the leaven means false teaching. For Luke, later, it will come to mean hypocrisy. But for Mark, it means poisoning or hardening of the heart.

Both the Pharisees and Herodians had sold their souls to vanity. They prided themselves in traditions, observances, and regulations, but they were not in tune with the faith that made those traditions possible. They carried within themselves daily, an infectious spirit that destroyed life. Had they been true to their own history, they would have understood that Jesus was feeding the multitude with bread through miracles that were the same as the ones employed by Moses and Elijah. Moses lifted his hands to God in prayer, and the Lord sent down bread from heaven. And Elijah with the hand of God used the last jar of meal and jug of oil that the widow of Zarephath had. And the last meal and oil lasted for many days until the Lord sent rain on the earth.

Because the Pharisees and Herodians were faithless, spiritless, and ruthless, Mark infers that there was no hope for them. Thus, Jesus' focus is on his disciples. Mark's emphasis is on the psychological and spiritual blindness of the disciples. Up to this point they had brought multitudes of hungry people to Jesus to feed. Twice he had fed them, in the previous passage and in Chapter 6. Yet the disciples missed the point. They should have known that Jesus can supply their needs from the "**one loaf**" on board with them or from nothing physically visible.

The second point in meditating on the loaf is not perceiving or recognizing it before their very eyes. Mark tells us in vs 14, "There is a loaf that's left over from the last feeding of the multitude." But Jesus the **Eternal Loaf** stands right there before their very eyes. And they failed to truly see him for what he really was. With all that had transpired before them and with all the words their ears had heard, their minds were still cloudy with heavy tread, because all that they worried about was physical bread. Now Jesus stands before them, for them, and on behalf of them as the Eternal Bread, the Bread of Life, the Bread from Heaven, and they do not see him. Mark goes on to complement the passage of the multiplication of loaves with the story of a blind man from Bethsaida whose friends brought him to Jesus and begged that Jesus heal him. Jesus took him by the hand, spit on his eyes, laid his hands on him, and asked him,

"Can you see anything?" And the man looked up and said, "I can see people, but they look like trees walking." Then Jesus laid his hands on him again; and he looked intently, and his sight was restored, and he saw everything clearly. Then Jesus sent him away to his home, saying, "Do not even go to the village." (NET Mark 8: 23-26)

Jesus' words in antiquity should resonate with many of us who are despairing because several of our children are still perishing in a starving land that indeed has bread. Why are you worried about having no bread? Do you not yet perceive or understand? Are your hearts hardened? Having eyes, do you not see, and having ears, do you not hear? Jesus the **Eternal Loaf,** purified, sanctified for humanity's wounded souls, completely unleavened, was broken one day on Calvary's mountain to make all of creation whole.

And so today, in our brokenness, hurts, and pains, in our short-sightedness amidst oil, rubber, and varieties of minerals in our land, in our infectious state of leaven, he invites all of us to become part of his mystical body, the spiritual loaf by symbolically/spiritually eating of the bread that was broken for us. How do I know? I heard the voice of Jesus saying, "I am the Bread of Life." I also heard him saying, "Come unto me all ye that are labored and heavy laden, and I'll give you rest."

In his classic, *Modern Man in Search of a Soul*, Carl Jung tells us that what distinguishes modern man from animals is when he is aware of his immediate present. In our text today, the Pharisees and Herodians, as the

Jungian analyst would put it, "lived in the animal kingdom with herds of pigs," because they were not aware of their present in living only within the bounds of tradition. They could have learned something from Father Abraham who was fully conscious and appreciative of the present. When the three angels Gabriel, Michael, and Raphael came to him at his tent in Hebron, Abraham embraced the future of God by faith.

The third point of meditation is the disciples forgetting the loaf. Jesus asked them, "And do you not remember? When I broke the five loaves for the five thousand, how many baskets full of broken pieces did you take up? They said to him 'twelve'. And for the four thousand, and they said to him, "seven". And he said to them, "Do you not yet remember?" We will never understand the dimness of the disciples' minds. Neither will we understand the reason for their spiritual sluggishness and despair until we search our own hearts.

What about ourselves? Are we not so slow to trust God and take the leap of faith in our personal lives? The disciples loved Jesus. But did they really know him? Blind Bartimaeus knew Jesus. When Bartimaeus heard that Jesus was passing by, he began to shout and say, "Jesus, Son of David, have mercy on me!" Many sternly ordered him to be quiet, but he cried out even more loudly, "Son of David, have mercy on me! Jesus asked, "What do you want me to do for you?" Bartimaeus replied, "My teacher, let me see again." Jesus said to him, "Go, your faith has made you well." Immediately, he regained his sight and followed him on the way. (GW Mark 10: 47-52) Bartimaeus' cognition was in order. His mere recognition that Jesus could heal him was indeed the curative factor.

Do we not yet remember? How quickly do many of us forget the immediate, decisive, and therapeutic/healing power of the **Loaf**. Every now and then we allow the troubles of this world to get hold of us. Every now and then, I too forget the one who saw me through, carried me through, and brought me through. Every now and then, like the disciples, I've forgotten the **Loaf** that stood by my side, and is standing by me right now. To those who are famished in Africa and the wider world, there is one who heals because he has and is the Bread of life. And because my situation was different, I can no longer afford to forget the one who was there for me when I was faced with high tuition payments. When I got down on my knees to pray, the **Loaf** fed me spiritually as I was hungry. It was that same loaf that provided bread in the form of spiritual strength, vision and the needed funds for my tuition. I cannot forget how Jesus the **Eternal Loaf** brought me out. He brought me out of my sorrows and shadows. He brought me out of the mired clay and set my feet on his Solid Rock of salvation. And that is why I love him so. In the words of Walter Hawkins:

> Dear Jesus, I love you
> You're a friend of mine.
> You supply my every need.
> My hungry soul you feed.

***Children at Fatima Elementary School, yearning
for spiritual and intellectual bread.***

2

Is There any Hope for Liberia?

We have discussed the problem of identity regarding the availability of bread in a starving land in the preceding chapter. In this segment we shall present some analysis in our attempt to find some solution to the problem of not finding it. In so doing, we ask rhetorically, "Is there any hope for Liberia?" And in order to begin an adequate response to this question, we shall take a retrospective glance at the formation of Liberia. Liberia was created experimentally within some cognitive dissonance (both positive & negative) of American political system in terms of slavery even before the end of the American Revolutionary War. The first man responsible for this idea of having a separate place/colony for free African slaves who were becoming a perceived threat to some Americans and the new Republic being founded was Thomas Jefferson, even though he was an embodiment of this paradox in view of the fact of him having some African mistresses and children. Liberia was also established as a de-facto US colony because of American geopolitical interests prompted by an awkward humiliation during the Libyan piracy of 1802 wherein Jefferson paid the ransom demanded by the Libyans in order to free American sailors off the coast of Tripoli.

However, it was President James Monroe who was responsible for the appropriation of money for the acquisition of land from the Bassa Chiefs and House Speaker Henry Clay, Lee and others from Virginia who subsequently acquired $250,000 from Congress to make this possible. Prompted by the Quakers, the American Colonization Society (ACS) led the voyage of discovery to Africa first in 1816 with Rev Jehudi Ashmun a Methodist minister, Bushrod Washington, a nephew of President George Washington, Thomas Buchanan who became the first Governor, and Joseph Jenkins Roberts the first African American[9] to be governor and subsequently president of the Republic of Liberia in 1847. Both Jefferson's cognitive dissonance and the benevolence of Monroe, Clay, and others above mentioned, fall within Jung's *Collective Unconscious* negatively and positively with these American revolutionaries having inherited their traits from their animal and human ancestors.

Robert Heilbroner, in *An Inquiry into the Human Prospect* asks, "Is there any hope for man?"[10] In the midst of moral decline, malaise, intolerance, indifference, cyclical asymmetry which spelled economic uncertainty, this question became central for Heilbroner in an American context. As the question became vital to this brilliant economist,

---

[9] Roberts can be called African American even though he was not an African but partially an African descent as a mulatto. He was neither an American because he became president of Liberia 18 years before the Emancipation Proclamation and accompanying amendments to the US Constitution.

[10] Heilbroner, New York, Pg.20

Heilbroner because it was an inquiry into the American state of mind, so is it with this writer, and thus, it is also an inquiry into the Liberian state of mind. In the face of economic stagnation and inflation (***stagflation***) for many Liberians who are experiencing high unemployment about 70%, high prices of essential commodities like rice, meat, flour, vegetables, drinking water, housing, and clothing, is there any hope for Liberia? Is there no balm in Gilead?

In his *Civilization and its Discontent,* Freud looks at the roots of discontent, the dark side of humanity as projected by the Nazis and the future of Nazi Germany. Freud speaks of the collective neurosis of the Nazis as they project themselves upon the Germans. Freud analyses Hitler's Germany/civilization to be the *superego* and the citizens to be the *id*. Discontent occurs because of the oppression by civilization and the repression of the *id/citizens*. Here in this work, we also feel impelled to look introspectively at the problem of discontent that is so rooted economically, psychologically, and spiritually in Liberia. What was the root cause of the physical, economic, and spiritual violence that wrecked the country into a civil war? Was it simply cultural divergence/ ethnocentrism as projected by some colonists/superego and experienced by the indigenous/id population? Was it false otherness, which was experienced not only within members of the "Americo-Liberians" entity like the Republican Party vs. True Whig Party and further schism within the True Whig Party as politicians collided but also the false otherness between the educated indigenous and non-educated indigenous Liberians? Or was it simply omnipotence, that deadly wish for power irrespective of ethnicity or skin color?

As Africans we are called by our creator to remove the mask of ethnicity in this lingering crisis in Liberia in order to see and understand the interplay between what Jacque Derrida calls *false otherness and real otherness.* When we remove this mask, we shall have some appreciation for the positive aspects of our collective pilgrimage in Liberia as a people. And without denying the savagery of our humanity in every ethnic group including the so-called "Americo- Liberians", we shall also affirm what kept majority of Liberians together for 175 + years and is now enabling them to seek an evolving process of integration.

In *Deconstruction in a Nutshell* Jacque Derrida defines *diffe`rance* as "a quasi -condition of possibility, because it does not describe fixed boundaries that delimit what can happen and what cannot, but points to its effects"[11] He goes on to describe how healing occurs in a colonial context, not because of the skills of the colonial medical practitioner but because of the *diffe`rance* between the doctor and the native patient. For Derrida, this is *real otherness. Real otherness* which is furthering the otherness of the other is responsible for bringing so many "Africo-Liberians" and "Americo-Liberians" together in *philos* and *eros* love over the years to the extent that it is almost impossible to identify a significant number of Liberians as "Americo" simply on their DNA structure.

False otherness, on the other hand, is extreme narcissism, colonialism, and ethnocentrism. It seeks to negate the humanity of the other. Jacques Derrida's deconstructionist/postmodernist thought is a direct response to the rampant xenophobia and its consequent prejudice of mainstream society upon people who are characterized as the "other." The critical task

---

[11] See Frank Caputo's *Deconstruction in a Nutshell on Jacques Derrida* **pg.102**

for Derrida, this Franco African, (Algerian Jew) master teacher and thinker, was how to deconstruct the alienating force experienced as "otherness"? Today as we continue to struggle with the mask of ethnic division and its pervasive hostility in Liberia, Derrida's task remains a challenge for us all. How do we as Africans get loose from Western bondage that is so obvious in our displaced aggression? When will we stop projecting our inner weakness and its resultant inner savagery upon our fellow Africans and Europeans who may appear different from us?

Like Derrida, this writer contends that it is only post-modern *diffe`rance* that can deconstruct the powers of colonialism, ethnocentrism, sexism, neo-colonialism, and narcissism whether they are in the form of apartheid (European created) or Liberian/Rwandan/CAR, and Burkina Faso savagery (African created).

Is there any hope for Liberia? In his *Phenomenology of Mind* Georg Hegel elucidates his dialectic of history that entails the tensions of slavery and freedom, suffering and atonement, and antithesis vs. synthesis to drive home the point that life is essentially a synthesis of opposites. This inner dialectic/duality connotes some absurdity of faith. Even if we were to employ some insights from the Hegelian dialectic in our anticipation of a better day in Liberia, in the face of some development projects underway by the Chinese, some European and American companies, Nigerians, and others, the question remains, is there any hope for Liberia? Implicit in this question is indeed a civilizational malaise. How is it that a country like ours that was once blessed with some visionary leaders, with economic imaginations, some of whom that the world will ever know, coupled with the fact, that the country is also rich in oil, iron ore, rubber, diamond, gold, and other commodities, is lagging seriously in seeing its citizens being happier or more content or richly developed as individual human beings? This civilizational malaise brings to consciousness the reality that the material and natural investments of a country are not enough to satisfy the human spirit. And with our immediate previous president having a wider sense of eco-justice, gender parity, compassion, and inclusion, why is it that many Liberians were and are still very nostalgic about a regime in our history that was ironically despotic and traumatic for others?

Is there any hope for Liberia? In this question we must sincerely ask whether we can imagine a future for Liberia other than a continuation of the darkness, cruelty, savagery, and disorder of our past. Here we can begin to address this problem introspectively by taking an inventory of our present anxiety, most specifically the collective neurosis experienced by many Liberians. Why is it so difficult for some Liberians to understand the root causes of ethnic and tribal divisions right at the formation of Liberia as a nation? Hope is not attainable without reconciliation. And there can be no reconciliation without the truth. No truth means no justice. And no justice means no reconciliation, which is perennial. As St Augustine of Hippo, Carthage/Tunisia asserted, "When justice is taken away, what are kingdoms but a vast banditry"? The presence of impunity spells the absence of accountability and thus the absence of justice. Justice is the precondition for reversing the permanence of anxiety (*angustia/angere*), the state wherein one is being choked mentally. Calvin says, "The anxious souls become their own executioners because they torment themselves by a lingering psychological death."[12] What are the roots of our current anxiety in the country? Did **Ebola** determine Liberia's destiny? As **Ebola** seems to be conquered, is it now becoming like the Greek god *Proteus* in having some of its roots/elements mutate into different forms? Are these roots also attributable to some *menaphim* (adulterers) who chased after the gods of vanity at the expense of the poor and nation's building despite President EJS' genuine efforts to curtail this economic injustice? And last, are the roots of anxiety in Liberia due to the inability of some of our people to produce bread in commensurate to the citizens of other Sub-Sahara African states like Cote D'Ivoire, Kenya, Ethiopia, Uganda, Ghana, and Nigeria? Walter Rauschenbusch shares some insight into the problem when he asserts:

> In a few years all our restless and angry hearts will be quiet in death, but those who come after us will live in the world which our sins have blighted or which our love of right has redeemed. Let us do our thinking on these great questions, not with our eyes fixed on bank accounts, but with a wise outlook on the field of the future and with the consciousness that the spirit of the Eternal is seeking to distill from our lives some essence of righteousness before they pass away.

At his eschatological (final) trial, in Plato's *Apologia Socratis,* Socrates concluded, "The unexamined life is a life not worth living for a human being. For unrighteousness runs deeper than death" (Plato, 399 BC). We can infer here that the unexamined station in life for anyone within

---

[12] See William Bousma's *John Calvin – A 16ᵗʰ Century Portrait*. See also *Calvin's Exegesis on Romans 8.*

Liberian society is not worth having. If we had cooperated with President EJS toward a genuine social reconstruction, Liberia could have averted its psychological dislocation, its regression into an economic abyss and reduced the wedge of inequality.

Is there any hope for Liberia? Amidst the dehumanization, physical and spiritual brutality caused by the existence and prevalence of idolatry, there is still hope. There is another side, an opposite to this psychological, physical, and spiritual death. That other side is life with God. The psychological breakthrough in Hebraic culture that ultimately and permanently leads to freedom and peace is summed in two Hebrew words **Avra** *(Ever)* *Ha* **Yadan**, beyond the Jordan. This is what Neway Debede means by **Alwashim** (free spirit). **Alwashim** means longing for freedom. Without the longing for freedom, which is rooted in the passion of God, we are nothing. This is also what Arthur Symons was alluding and explicating when his soul cried out, and Dubois' soul echoed that cry,

> O water, voice of my heart, crying in the sand,
> All night long crying with a mournful cry,
> As I lie and listen and cannot understand
> The voice of my heart in my side or the voice of the sea,
> O water, crying for rest, is it I, is it I?
> All night long the water is crying to me.

Was the voice of the sea protesting in crying because both the black and white races were responsible for throwing several African slaves especially women overboard the **Tecora** and finally shipping the rest of them to the Americas during the Transatlantic Slavery? And is the voice of the sea still protesting in crying to the rest of us in prompting us to do our very best in obliterating all forms of slavery in this present age? In antiquity the Jordan River symbolized physical and spiritual death. Yet Almighty God instructed Elijah to strike the waters of the Jordan with his mantle whereby the river was parted into two, and he and his spiritual son Elisha were able to cross on dry land.

Prior to Elijah and Elisha crossing the Jordan, the Lord afflicted and killed King Ahaziah of Samaria for worshipping BaalZebub, the god of Ekron. Also, prior to crossing the Jordan, as the land was barren, and there were no fruits and vegetation, and the water was contaminated, the Spirit of God instructed Elijah to apply salt in the water and the land was healed. Amidst the severity of human suffering in Liberia caused mainly by the pervasiveness of many people in their ignorance of worshipping so many idols of oppression, materialism, and political figures, there is still hope. For God himself will destroy the principal idol worshippers. Again, *Avra yadan* (beyond the Jordan) reminds us that there is another side, an opposite of fear and death, which is life.

Is there hope for Liberia? Elsewhere in 2 Chronicles 7:14, King Solomon is instructed by Yahweh (Adonai) to assert, "If my people, which are called by my name, shall humble themselves, pray and seek my face and turn from their wicked ways, then will I hear from heaven, and heal their land." Is there hope for Liberia? First, the Tiawan Gongloe-oriented Broom to sweep corruption, which he got from Amos Claudius Sawyer, his former boss four decades ago, must be implemented now to clean the collective soul of Liberia and not in some distant political future. This effort should entail the Liberian Council of Churches and Interfaith Council, and the President of Liberia leading the nation in regular disciplines of spiritual self-humiliation of prayer and fasting. What the Liberian people need is

Reconciliation now among themselves and not Retribution from a future ruling tribe or political party.

Next, with all the funds that are being raised by political parties in the diaspora, it is time for the government, opposition political parties along with Civil Society and human rights organizations to participate in shared governance in order to allocate resources now for the Liberian people instead of waiting until January 2024. Purposely, a joint-task force must strive for economic reconversion (readjustment) that enables micro-financing for marketeers especially women, which similarly was implemented by former CBL Governor Dr. J. Mills Jones. In view of this, we are appreciative of Alexander Cummings' moral courage in supporting institutions of redemption. Here Cummings' efforts can be complemented by Joe Boakai's skills in agricultural development and Sen Karnga-Lawrence's effort, courage, and passionate heart for all Liberians. But Cummings should desist from denigrating President Weah. Every time he cusses the president, he diminishes himself and Liberia. He must respect the President.

Additionally, and critically, basic tenets of Thorstein Veblen's economics on personal growth and his warning on **conspicuous consumption** must be accentuated and appropriated to the masses. For a people to humble themselves before God their maker, some of their leaders in various government ministries should not boast about not "being caught dead" driving a regular SUV or shopping at stores that ordinary people shop at when they are in the Diaspora, especially when some of these officials are stealing the money from the Liberian tax- payers. That kind of conspicuous consumption (corruption) inflames everlasting hatred.

Third, basic tenets from Jeffrey Sachs' *The End of Poverty: Economic Possibilities for our Time* should be utilized by the collaborative force of the Liberian government, its opposition political parties, Civil Society, and other stake holders. Sachs focuses on **"clinical economics"**, which rejects the IMF's austerity measures for many poor countries. He also draws attention on bad governance, which hinders infrastructure development and total economic growth, and climate change, which has a disproportionate impact on underdeveloped nations.

Lastly, basic tenets from Joseph Schumpeter's *Creative Destruction* (Innovation) should be carefully understood, appreciated, and appropriated. In his trailblazing work, Schumpeter shows us how "industrial mutation transforms economic structure from within, eliminating the old one and creating a new one" (Schumpeter, 1942). This was what Frantz Fanon meant when he asserted that "true independence produces the spiritual and material conditions for the reconversion of man" (Fanon, 1963). Equally monumental, was Fanon's point of departure, which became a tour de force, that "the inner mutation, the renewal of the social and family structures that impose with the rigor of the law lead to the emergence of the nation and the growth of its sovereignty" (Fanon, 1963). When we look at young and old Ethiopian artists as entrepreneurs in synthesizing the flute, masenqo, drums, and other traditional instruments in the process of mutating and streaming new methods of videos and replacing the old ones, and utilizing special threads and leathers for weaving bags, shoes, sweaters, and sandals tantamount to what Dolly Barnes did with some women at Grand Cavalla, Maryland, then surely, they as entrepreneurs are part of the economic community of innovations.

Is there any hope for Liberia? Illegal commodities possibly flowing on the waters of Africa's Maryland in the absence of Coast Guards pose a serious terrorist threat to the nation. T.S. Eliot says, "For us, there is only trying, the rest is not our business" (1942). In God's will is our peace. "Wheat must be crushed before it becomes bread", says Ruth Barnes Baker. Our wounds are healed through the wounds of Calvary. And in his affirmation amidst the 17th century Interregnum in Great Britain, that great Anglican divine, Jeremy Taylor asserted, "Circumstances cannot overcome someone who is content…whenever we suffer for a good cause, even when we fall down, we are not destroyed…To have God's friendship is everything." There is hope. For there is balm (healing plant) in Gilead. Moreover, the Calvary event through Christ made the spiritual passage through the Jordan possible for believers at the end of their physical life. It also means that amidst the dehumanization, systemic marginalization, and starvation that are attributable to massive corruption, there is an opposite, another side of this psychological death. And it is life with God. There is hope.

Therefore, from the Cape of Palms and Sheppard Lake in Africa's Maryland to Montserrado's lofty heights, to Cape Mount and its Pisco Lake, from Maryland's Kaduwe and Swe Mountains to Mount Wologizi, from Mount Nimba to Grand Gedeh's Bauni Mountain, there's an *Eternal Voice* that calls us to seek the *Eternal Loaf* by praying,

> Our Father who art in heaven; hallowed be thy name, thy kingdom come. Thy will be done on earth as it is in heaven. Give us this day our daily bread. Lead us not into temptation but deliver us from evil. Amen.

Going to God through Christ yields true psychological liberation as the believer feels a liberating dependence upon God for daily bread. For in prayer the priority is the glory of God and his kingdom. Elsewhere, Jesus says, "Seek ye first the kingdom of God and his righteousness and all things will be added." (Matthew 6: 33) This prayer of Jesus, which is modeled after the Jewish Kiddish, frees us from ***diffidentia*** (mistrust) because the moment we call God father the doors of heaven are open to us. And all things including principalities and powers are subject to the sovereignty of our heavenly father.

Even though the acquisition of daily bread or bread for the coming day is of critical importance, here, attaining it without seeking reconciliation/ psychological liberation first with God is in vain. As David in dedication to Solomon in the 127 Psalm reminds us, "It is vain for anybody in hastening to rise early, to go late at rest, to eat the bread of sorrows." Echoing David, Calvin says, "Bread of sorrows means what one acquires by hard and anxious labor or what is eaten with disquietude of mind."[13] Also, my Professor at UNC Chapel Hill during the mid-1990's, Peter Kaufman impressed upon us that Calvin employed his political theology to make Geneva a model Christian Community (God's government on earth). Thus, for this writer, even greater than Constantine who exploited the Cross (Meskel) in furthering his goal as an imperialist, Calvin, as a liberationist brought to fruition political and religious redemption in Geneva, Switzerland. That is why Jesus shapes the priority by having the disciples to first pray for the glory of God and then second to seek other things including physical bread.

13

As indicated earlier, Jung's explication of modern man finds resonance with me. Unlike Nietzsche whose sagacity of modern man is one that goes with the flow sometimes as a complacent member of the "herd of man who lacks exceptional spiritual health," Jung's modern man "stands upon a peak or at the very edge of the world, the abyss of the future before him, above him the heavens, and below him the whole of mankind with a history that disappears in primeval mists" (Jung, 1933)

So just where can modern man turn for life and the bread to sustain that life? Where can Africa turn for life and the bread to preserve its life? Bread can be found in the ***unconscious*** as Socrates, Plato, Sophocles, the prophets of Israel, and Jesus explicated that truth was rooted in the unconscious. And Fanon asserted that truth/bread can be found in the ***African unconscious***. Africa, especially Liberia, must remember the traditional Hebrews who in their **HaMotzi** blessing prayed, "Blessed art thou, O Lord, God of the universe who brings forth bread from the heavens (shamayim)". We must also remember Luther as he says, in seeking bread for the coming day, let us set our eyes not only at the oven but also toward the distant field and the entire land, which bears and brings to us daily every sort of sustenance. Here, Luther reminds us that it is only God who causes the grain to grow and blesses and preserves it in the field. Without this, there could be no bread in the oven and upon the table.

Is there any hope for Liberia? There is a serious deficiency in cognitive development, moral and faith development, and psychosocial development here among some Liberian youths who know nothing better because they are part of the culture of violence as the result of being nurtured by their idols of wars. Yet we cannot afford to answer the question without looking at some progress former President EJS and her educational team made in light of the expansion of the University of Liberia at Fendell and at Sanji, Grand Cape Mount County during the administration of Dr. Emmett Dennis, at one of the best systems of education in Liberia at Stella Maris Poly-technical College via Sister Laurent Brown, with some excellent programs in Gender and Development, farms at Barrobo and Cavalla at Tubman University in Maryland during the administration of Dr. Elizabeth Davis-Russell along with Marylanders for Progress in the USA, the expansion of AMEU, AMEZU, CU, UMU, and the formation of additional community colleges nationwide. Amidst the systemic marginalization and dehumanization of women in Liberia, other parts of Africa, and other global villages by truncating their politically collective voice, and the lingering problem of raping little girls by psychopaths in an insouciant political culture, we must be highly appreciative for the establishment of The EJS Presidential Center for Women and Development. We must also appreciate the sophisticated banking system that President Sirleaf put in place to the extent that Liberia was respected highly by the World Bank and IMF. In so doing, let us laud some efforts/mechanisms of transparency and anti-corruption commissions that she instituted.

And finally, we must juxtapose the modernization of Monrovia in its infrastructure efforts with its problem of congested population. Here we must appreciate former President Sirleaf as she shared her vision in extending development beyond Monrovia and Ganta to marginalized areas of the country. Reinvestment contingencies in the Ports of Harper, Greenville, and Buchanan as well as enabling a viable superhighway from Maryland to Monrovia via the coastline will enhance the legacy of her presidency and help the current government in uniting the country.

As we have elucidated that there is hope because of the existence of bread in a starving Africa, we are also asserting that it is attainable by music and dancing. which are part of the sensory apparatus.

3

Self-transcendence through Music and Dancing

Music is a moral law.
It gives soul to the universe,
Wings to the mind, and
Charm and gaiety to life. (Schopenhauer)

Musically, even the country's *Lone Star Forever* has an emotional resonance. 114 years ago, Edwin James Barclay anticipated Liberia's perennial inner struggle between hope and despair when he wrote:

When Freedom raised her glowing form
On Montserrado's verdant height,
She set the dome of night,
The Star of Liberty!
And seizing from the waking morn,
Its burnished shield of golden flame,
She lifted it in her proud name,
And roused a nation long forlorn,
To nobler destiny!

It is our hope that Liberians will forever be grateful to President Barclay who was 19 years old at the time of his composition and to Almighty God for such inspiration. For every day of freedom is an act of faith as the ancient Hebrews posited. In the Amharic language of Ethiopia, the word, *mulu* means whole. Thus, we agree with Schopenhauer that music is the essence and existence of life. For in our search for the wholeness (loaf) of intellectual and spiritual bread, it is music that takes us higher. Music is the artist's will to power and possibilities.

The song "Mary Don't You Weep" that several Gospel artists sang, points to the God of liberation in what He did to and for the Hebrew slaves musically, in giving them Songs in the night by parting the Red Sea during the night and drowning Pharaoh's armies. "All that night the Lord drove the sea back with a strong east wind and turned it into dry land." (Exodus 14:21) It became a music that would last forever. Arthur Schopenhauer once averred that music expresses our will to power as it depicts a better reality of a world to be transformed. In his *"The World as Will and Representation,"* Schopenhauer felt that music was the key in the perceptual capacity of the soul (Aristotelian). He also focused on eternal justice. Schopenhauer emphasizes:

> In music we do not recognize the repetition of any idea of
> the inner nature of the world. Yet it is such a great art, its
> effect on man's innermost nature is so powerful and is
> understood by him in his innermost being as an
> entirely universal language.

In the case of James Brown and other musicians who as children and adolescents were abused and abandoned by their biological parents, life itself became music. Thus, in learning and playing the notes of life as young musicians, they were able to transcend their despised conditions and contribute to the ecstatic joy of the world. For Schopenhauer, music is the highest form of all arts. His philosophy of music is captured on *Wille Zum Leben*, the will to live. Music enhances our will to live. Focusing on *Wille Zum Leben*, Schopenhauer highly accentuated, "Are not the mountains, waves, and skies, a part of me and my soul, as I of them"? He further underscores, "When we listen to music, we feel as though we instantly connect with a higher truth" (Schopenhauer, 1818). From his movie studio Isaac Hayes says it best when he avers,

> If the music makes you move
> cause you can dig the groove
> Then groove on
> Groove on
> If you feel like you wanna say
> And talking is the only way
> Rap on
> Ah rap on
> Cause whatever oh you do
> Oh, you've got to do your thing yah.

We cannot engage in any serious discussion of Music without some depth of retrospective appreciation for my own dad, Theodore Momolu Gardiner, Sr. and uncle S. Faikai Gardiner, Sr. My dad introduced me to the music of Beethoven, Johann Sebastian Bach, and Martin Luther. Luther defines music as "a divine gift that appears throughout nature but reaches its perfection in human beings" (Luther, 1538). His *A Mighty Fortress is our God* was extrapolated from Psalm 46. "And though this world with devils filled, should threaten to undo us, we will not fear, for God has willed his truth to triumph through us." For Luther, music destroys the power of the devil and throws away the effects of melancholia. It has been in this spirit of self-transcendence that we have seen emerging the extraordinary musical dexterity of Winder and Joydne Harmon. Winder and Joydne have made music accessible as spiritual, psychological, and intellectual bread for their brothers and sisters in a starving Africa. In their classic production they illuminate **the faithfulness of God** (Romans 8: 31-39), in pouring out their hearts, "We've got to praise You for being so faithful Lord." Also, Hakal Cooper, Jordi Kiadii, and Francis Gardiner, three young musicians whose skills on the organ, guitar, and violin respectively, are directly inherited from their great-grandfather and grandfather, Theodore Momolu Gardiner, Sr.

Uncle Faikai perfected Francis Lyte's song of prayer, *"Abide with me fast Falls the eventide."* There was nobody in the entire Republic of Liberia that could play that song instrumentally like my late uncle. Ironically, Lyte wrote that song in the same year of Liberia's Independence through which he was calling upon Almighty God to abide with him throughout his life as he was struggling and dying from tuberculosis. Another song that Heaven graced uncle Faikai's fingers with was:

> Bread of the world in mercy broken,
> wine of the soul in mercy shed,
> by whom the words of life were spoken,
> and in whose death our sins are dead.

Uncle Faikai would first play the song instrumentally. Then my dad Theodore, a musical genius in arranging notes, who on occasions as a harpist and organist had played culturally with Briggs Cummings and Lawrence Andrews, would then join my mother Lucinda, Annie Hamilton,

Susannah Morais, David Freeman, Melita Cummings, Joe Diggs, Jaima Gray, Sarah Pearson, and others in singing further, (Bread of the world*)*

Look on the heart by sorrow broken
look on the tears by sinners shed,
and by thy feast to us the token
that by thy grace our souls are fed.

Still more sacred of the Anglican music is, *"The King of Love my Shepherd is"*, which is an extrapolation of Psalm 23. Both my dad and Uncle Faikai played it very well. The goodness of the King faileth never; We nothing lack if we are his. Where streams of living water flow, my ransomed soul he leadeth. And where the verdant pastures grow with food celestial feedeth. The song depicts the love of the Shepherd, the love shown by both earthly and heavenly fathers in picking up their children.

We have discussed how music as bread is self-transcending. Now let us see how dancing is also self-transcending. What exactly is dancing? Dancing is overcoming oneself, coming to term with one's inadequacy and surrendering it to the sufficiency of a higher power. For the believer, that greater power is God. Self-transcendence is digging deeply into one's innermost self and transforming everything in it including fear, greed, selfishness, hatred, and pride and prejudice.

Friederich Nietzsche defines life as a dance. Amidst the suppression of dance by many "Christians" during the 19th century, he asserted that dance was an interpretive key in understanding how to overcome oneself and remain faithful to this sacred earth. In his work, *The Birth of Tragedy*, Nietzsche says, as rhythms move people to feel joy, they also help in shaping their destiny. And their bodily selves as catalysts are monumental in overcoming oneself for wholistic transformation. We find this Phenomenon with the Ethiopians collectively and other artists individually from other parts of Africa and the United States of America. Through dancing, the bodily movements of most Ethiopians affect their subconscious in reaching their sensory apparatus in igniting the perceptual capacity of their souls, which enables dexterities and other creative possibilities.

Nietzsche in *Human All Too Human* argues, "When humans don't learn to move their bodily selves, their senses grow dull, and they lose the capacity to discern what is good for them." For him, dance was a joyful affirmation of life. Dance illustrated a higher and greater intelligence in yielding a creative art of music with fruits of love and harmony while doing away with resentment and the need for revenge. In imitating Zarathustra, the prophet of monotheistic Zoroastrianism, Nietzsche asserted that God dances as He liberates his creation especially nature. For Zarathustra emphasizes:

You ubermen/ higher men, the worst about you is that you have not learned to dance away over yourselves! What does it matter that you are failures? How much is still possible.

Also, from Zarathustra, Nietzsche underscores in *Human, All Too Human* that the first step in this vital transformation, is "becoming a free spirit and be willing to step outside of one's comfort zone to carry heavy weights and sacrifices oneself. That means, man must injure his pride, to let his folly shine out in order to mock his wisdom" (Nietzsche, 1879). The above mentioned Nietzschean insight ironically parallels Augustinian-Calvinistic thought. For self-liberation entails "building the bridge on which you, and only you, must cross over the river of life" (Nietzsche, 1872)

In *The Antichrist* (1895), Nietzsche reminded the world how "dance was a discipline for training sensory awareness and cultivating skills of perception and responsibility." It was in this light of Nietzsche's perspective of self-transcendence in insisting that "our highest goals must affirm bodily life," that even Presidents Bill Clinton, George W. Bush, and Barack Obama danced publicly. And despite his childhood traumatic experience of parental abuse and abandonment, James Brown was able to overcome, transcend himself (Nietzschean) through his bodily movements. His God-given art creatively enabled him to produce one of the best songs of all time *This is a Man's World*. In that song, he synthesized tenor and alto saxophones with syncopation from his singers and dancers, which yielded ecstatic joy and love.

Rev, President Garretson W. Gibson

Rev Alexander Crummell

Bishop Samuel D. Ferguson

Bishop Theophilus M. Gardiner

4

Enabling Spiritual and Intellectual Bread via the American Missionary Efforts of The Reverend (President) Garretson Wilmot Gibson, Reverend Alexander Crummell, The Right Reverend Samuel David Ferguson, and The Right Reverend Theophilus Momolu Fiker Gardiner

In the history of the development of the Episcopal Church of Liberia, all routes led to Cape Palmas, Maryland. A vibrant intellectual and spiritual life began for the young Garretson Wilmot Gibson who landed in Cape Palmas with his parents on the ship, Schooner Harmony in 1845 from Baltimore, Maryland, U.S.A. Antecedent to Gibson's pilgrimage to Cape Palmas was the missionary voyage of Bishop John Payne in 1841. (Dunn, 1992)

Upon his entry into Liberia, Gibson at age 13, studied at the Episcopal Mission school at Mt. Vaughan, which also became known as Tubman Town that was founded by manumitted slaves of Richard and Emily Tubman of Augusta, Georgia in 1844. Gibson studied under the tutelage of Dr. George A. Perkins. He also gained some educational proficiency later under Bishop John Payne who was consecrated Bishop of Cape Palmas and Parts Adjacent in West Africa by the Episcopal Church of the United States of America (ECUSA) in 1851 (Dunn, 1992).

Subsequently, Gibson returned to Baltimore in order to enhance his studies in Theology for two years. Ultimately, he returned to Harper where he was ordained a priest in 1853 at St. Mark's the first Parish in the nation (with Epiphany in Cavalla being the first Episcopal Ministry). Immediately upon his ordination as priest, Gibson simultaneously served as Assistant Minister of St. Mark's Church and Principal of Mt. Vaughan High School at Tubman Town. "Ten years later he became Rector of Trinity Church in Monrovia where he served for twenty years" (Dunn, 2010).

As a vibrant and committed scholar and pastor in service to humanity, Gibson provided sustenance of intellectual and spiritual bread in both secular (political) and religious dimensions of life. What a great intellect he was, "laboring as Commissioner of Education, Professor at Liberia College, and serving concurrently as President Gardiner's Secretary of State and President of Liberia College" (Brawley, 1921 and Dunn, 2001).

And during the period of national discontent appertaining to the payment of gold duties, he asserted, "The citizens of Liberia are entitled to know what becomes of every dollar that is paid into the Government Treasury, and the laws of the State have made the necessary provision for them to have this information" (ACS, 1901).

Apparently, Gibson knew himself. And he understood his people in Liberia. Moreover, he understood his dual calling by his Maker. After his tenure as President of the Republic, he humbly and faithfully continued to serve the Episcopal Church of Liberia in Cape Mount and other areas of the country. Also, with strong diplomatic skills, he was willing to join the Liberian delegation under the Arthur Barclay administration in travelling to Europe in order to negotiate development assistance for his country. Thus, with qualitative efficacy, he enabled spiritual and intellectual bread in Liberia, a starving Africa. And one of his progeny, Henry Reid Cooper became a Chief Justice of the Supreme Court of Liberia 93 years later upon his death in 1910.

Sometime around his late teen years, another young man emerged but was faced with the reality of segregation and racial aversion. This reality prompted him to seek his educational objectives through an abolitionist institution in New Hampshire. But such alternative path to his education was annihilated when a racist community demolished the school. Such destruction and dehumanization sprouted hatred, despair, and doubt (Dubois, 1903) in the mind of young Alexander Crummell, which was lingering in his life for a considerable time. Amidst such a major setback, which was very traumatic for Crummell, Bariah Greene threw him a life jacket by educating him in Oneida, New York at a white school, which diminished some of the hatred. Still Crummell was rejected by the Apostolic Church of God because he was a negro. "And he blamed the world for this injustice." (Anderson, 1998).

Nevertheless, Crummell was educated informally at Yale by some sympathetic lecturers. "For a while his congregation flourished, but then people stopped attending church. Here, despair turned into doubt. He began to doubt the capability of the African American race and of his own vocation" (Anderson, 1998). Consequently, he began to believe that he had failed. Did Crummell really understand himself, his own African American community, and Africa itself? Was he resilient as a scholar and pastor but deficient as a leader both politically and ecclesiastically? As he viewed the educational ministry in Liberia, only African American educators in the States had the requisite dexterities and modern analytical tools for a one-way assimilation with the specific focus of "civilizing mission" of Christianity. Like many negroes in America, despite enduring painful rejection in his desire to be trained in some American divinity schools, Crummell wanted to completely acculturate African mission stations into Western traditions. Says Tibebu, "Crummell wanted Africans to become Europeanized" (Tibebu, 2012).

Crummell moved to Liberia via Cape Palmas sixteen years after Bishop Payne had settled and solidified his ministry in Cape Palmas and two years after Bishop Payne was consecrated by the House of Bishops as Bishop of Cape Palmas and Parts Adjacent in Africa. Yet Crummell was often incongruous and discourteous with his supervisor, Bishop Payne. He attempted to start a new Diocese in Monrovia. What was going on? Was this a reemergence of inferiority that began with racial hatred in America now manifesting itself in Africa? Crummell who was once brought to degradation by a white Bishop in Philadelphia now finds himself in the presence of another white Bishop in Africa, only this time, in the eyes of others, it is anticipative for him to engage in genuine Christian, self-humiliation and healing for the sake of the kingdom.

Bishop Payne was formally educated at the 2nd institution of higher learning to be founded in the U.S., the College of William and Mary (Episcopalian) plus Virginia Theological Seminary while Crummell was denied admission at General Theological Seminary (Episcopalian) because he was black. Nevertheless, Crummell was informally educated at the 3rd College to be founded in the U.S., Yale College plus further training at Cambridge University in England. What was going on in Crummell's horizon? Did he feel some sense of inferiority and hostility in view of what Dubois called "double- consciousness" (psychological tension of African Americans conforming to a white culture in one black body)? Despite the distinctive educational experiences of Bishop Payne and Crummell, no school is ever so low or so high to be far remote from the blessings, the Eternal Bread of God. And despite the antinomies by Crummell and some other black Americans, how could they "Christianize and civilize" Africa? Did Crummell know Africans? Did he understand them? Was he genuine at all? How could a group of settlers and its counterpart the American Colonization Society in the early to mid-19th century, "civilize" an African continent, when Islam which emphasizes in its Koran that Jesus (Isa) is the Messiah (al Masiah), and as a Prophet (nabi) performing several miracles, He became one of God's greatest creations, had already had a ***Civilizing Influence*** in Africa thru Emperor Mansa Musa of the ancient Kingdoms of Ghana, Mali, and Songhai during the 14th century? Also, King Sao Boso Kamara (Botswain), a political genius, liberator, and a devout Islamic cleric (Iman) provided timely military intervention for the ACS' settlement around Cape Mesurado amidst the 1822 crisis during the governance of Rev Jehudi Ashmun. As a major founding father of Liberia, King Boso Kamara set the stage for Roberts, Warner, Teague, Gardiner, and Blyden.

Nevertheless, Christianity has always had a ***Civilizing Influence*** in all countries of the world. And some of Liberia's great emancipators above-mentioned like Joseph Jenkins Roberts, Hilary Teague, Daniel Bashiel Warner, Anthony William Gardiner, and Edward Wilmot Blyden, in addition to understanding the history of the building of the great Pyramids of Egypt, which was a signifier of one of the world's best civilizations, knew and felt the power of Christianity. But our beloved missionaries, especially Crummell, neglected to mention the ***Civilizing Influence*** of 6th Century Christianity in the **Kingdoms of Axum, Gondar, and Lalibela Ethiopia** (Abyssinia) where justice was the soul of the empire.

Still, Crummell was an intellectual giant who greatly impacted Liberian intellectual and spiritual life at Caldwell and when he served as Professor of Philosophy and English at Liberia College. But his rhetoric of "pure black" in superficially identifying with the indigenes backfired as power was still concentrated within the mulatto enclave that wanted diversity without the versatility of an indigene presidency. Thus, he ultimately became a clear and present danger to himself and the Liberian government, which necessitated his departure from Liberia in 1875. Upon his return to the States, he co-founded the famed St. Luke's Episcopal Church which was the first independent church for black Episcopalians in Washington, D.C. And antecedent to Carter G. Woodson, Crummell taught at Howard University. He founded the American Negro Academy in D.C. one year before his death. And prior to that he founded Pan Africanism along with Martin Delaney sixty years before Dubois, Nkrumah, and George Padmore celebrated it at Manchester, England in 1945. Alexander Crummell and his friend Henry Highland Garnet attended the African Free School in New York at the outset of their educational journey. But unlike Crummell, Garnet who was U.S. Presbyterian Minister and diplomat to Liberia was treated like Liberia's very own. Garnet seemed to have understood Africans very well especially since his critical lineage flowed back to the great warrior and African chief, his grandfather who was betrayed, captured, and sold to slave traders. The Liberian government and people of Liberia loved Garnet. President Hilary Richard Wright Johnson and the Liberian people gave him a State Funeral when he died. He was buried like an African prince in Monrovia with Edward Wilmot Blyden eulogizing him on February 13, 1882.

The Right Reverend Samuel David Ferguson moved to Cape Palmas, Liberia with his parents when he was six years old, one year after Liberia's Independence from the American Colonization Society. Apparently, he attended the Episcopal mission school at Mount Vaughan, Tubman Town. Like Garretson Gibson antecedent to him, Ferguson labored first as Assistant Minister then subsequently as Rector of St. Mark's Episcopal Church. He enabled intellectual and spiritual bread by envisaging and founding "Cuttington Collegiate and Divinity School, the Julia C. Emery School and countless other schools in local villages" (Dunn, 1992). With James Theodore Holley a Washington, D.C. born clergy as the first African American Bishop in the Protestant Episcopal Church, Ferguson was the second African American to become a member of the House of Bishops.

Clearly, as a proponent of a two-way assimilation of cultures in shaping the Republic, Ferguson, consequentially, made a tremendous impact in enhancing the attainability of intellectual and spiritual bread in a starving Africa. "With a $5,000 gift from Robert F. Cutting, Ferguson established the 100 acres of land school with an all- Liberian staff...The departments entailed theological, agricultural, and industrial education" (Dunn, 1992).

Ferguson's vision for Cuttington was empowering the youths of Liberia and Africa with the requisite dexterities in order to provide physical sustenance that were germane to the needs of a developing nation. With the exception of Henry Too Wesley, a very light skin indigene from Fish Town, Maryland, who attended Cuttington and Liberia Colleges and ultimately became the 19th Vice-President of Liberia, Arthur Barclay's administration ill-treated many coastal indigenous people. Ferguson strongly condemned this repugnance because ministers were watchmen on the walls. (Ezekiel 3) Under Ferguson's leadership, many indigenous teachers and clergy increased. He also taught many personages who emigrated from the State of Maryland in the USA like James Hilary Dennis but drew no distinction among both groups (Cooper, 1996). Also, Ferguson educated and ordained Randolph and Colston Cooper. Moreover, he educated Deacons Theophilus M. Gardiner, Pearson and others to the priesthood. Randolph Cooper married Bishop Ferguson's daughter, Cynthia, but sustained the untimely death of her (Cooper, 1996). Unequivocally, Ferguson staunchly felt that the rigid dichotomy between the indigenes and America-Liberians could be healed through what Plato called *Paideia* (industrial, religious, and agricultural education). He revitalized the Bromley mission for girls. Under him, the Episcopal Church took the lead in educating more "native" students than government schools (Dunn, 1992 and Anderson, 1998).

Bishop Theophilus Momolu Fiker Gardiner enabled spiritual and intellectual bread in Liberia as he strived for harmony of the nation by facilitating peace among various ethnic tribes in the South-Eastern region of Liberia. Gardiner also opted for a two-way assimilation in being authentic to the redemption of the soul of Liberia. Gardiner, as

44

Africa's first Episcopal Bishop in Liberia, became one of the long awaited Deutero Isaiah's suffering-type servants. Immediately upon his election in 1921 by the Episcopal Church in New York, the US House of Bishops wired a telegram to Chief Justice James Jenkins Dossen who personally delivered the correspondence to him. Like Aeschylus in antiquity, Gardiner understood that growth comes through suffering.

Prior to being elected as Bishop, Gardiner labored assiduously as President of the Council of Advice in the Missionary District of Liberia of the Episcopal Church. Because "he was a member of the Vai tribe and a former Muslim, his consecration as bishop was an inspiration to many church people in Liberia" (Dunn, 1992). Also, precursory to his election and consecration as bishop, as a committed scholar who enabled intellectual and spiritual bread, Gardiner labored diligently as Professor of History of World Civilizations and Patristics, which entailed Christianity in Antiquity and Medieval Church History. In this discipline, he also taught Patristic Latin, Greek, and Hebrew at Cuttington Collegiate and Divinity School to future leaders and educators. Bishop Gardiner saw his flock as souls in scattered missions. Thus, the Divinity propelled him to enter deep into the brokenness of their humanity to encounter their pain and anguish in places like Sodoken, Kaloqen, Barrobo, Gedetarbo, Webbo, Cavalla, Rocktown, Fishtown, Grandcess, Sasstown, Sinoe, Bassa, Cape Mount, and Monrovia. And despite the American Church's resistance to the influence of African culture in its Christian mission of ecclesiastical and educational dimensions, Gardiner courageously ventured into the depth culture of Liberia with its rich intellectual and spiritual reservoir in order to guide his flock back to the Lover and Keeper of their souls.

On many Saturday mornings, many residents of Harper and surrounding areas like Hoffman Station would gather at the Gardiner residence to receive various modes od physical bread for sustenance. According to the New York Times article, "T.M. Gardiner, 71 Bishop of Liberia," Gardiner rejected his family's offer to be the direct heir of the (Massaquois) estate of farms and lands and servants. Instead, he ventured on "long, hard trips via land and sea, building mission stations" (NY Times, 1941). Gardiner also mediated the courage to be full persons (neither inferior nor superior) to both the upper class and "subaltern class" (Kieh, 2017) of Liberia. He addressed their humanity. Such mediation included bringing existential hope to the "wretched of the earth" (Fanon) in Liberia by also furthering their inner harmony (eudaimonia). For this reason, both Presidents Charles Dunbar King and Edwin James Barclay sat at his feet in seeking his advice during their time of distress and its consequential spiritual and political diffidence upon them in order to gain the needed confidence to continue governing. Also, for this reason, Gardiner was "Knighted in the Humane Order of African Redemption by the President of Liberia" (NY Times, 1941). As an educator in service of the soul of Liberia, "Liberia College conferred upon him the Doctor of Divinity degree" (NY Times, 1941). Born in Dearlah, Cape Mount, he was the son of Tarweh (Guarnyar) and Momolu Fiker Gardiner. He was married to Ms. F Rebecca Neal. They had one son, Frank Gardiner. When she passed away, he married Danielette Francis Wilson. Together they successfully raised Frank, Sammy, Theodore, Cecelia, Danielette, and Faikai.

Throughout the above-mentioned missionary journey, the efforts of enabling intellectual and spiritual bread to the wretched of the earth were not easy. There were hurdles along the way. But it was the melody of love that came from Heaven above, which mediated existential hope to all ethnic groups in encouraging them to fly with wings of a dove in sharing their common humanity. Dr. Elwood Dunn best stated that it was the people and culture of Liberia that shaped the style of the Church of Liberia.

Harper, Cape Palmas outside of St. Mark's Episcopal Church

Kingdom of Lalibela, Ethiopia

Kingdom of Gondar, Ethiopia

Kingdom of Axum, Ethiopia

5

In Her Darkness

In her darkness that was triggered by severe ignorance and wretchedness, Liberia a Starving Africa cried for bread but found none beginning in 1977. President Tolbert was a good man and an economic visionary. But despite my deep appreciation for Tolbert's *From Mat-to-Mattress* emphasis, religious/Pharisaical zealotry, a dangerous idolatry wherein one's sees his interpretation of the *nomos* (law) as God, prompted his anxious soul to hastily signed his own (foster) brother's death warrant within few months of becoming president. Additionally, his Minister of Justice, Oliver Bright deceived him into unlawfully executing Superintendent James Anderson and Mr. Seton of Maryland County in 1978 in a case with ***reasonable doubt*** (**lack of preponderance of evidence**) that was predicated on the political insecurities of Bright and Tolbert. Regardless of any affiliation, truth is the precondition for reconciliation as it is the centrality of the Constitution in any respectable society. The government of Liberia disregarded Aristotelian justice, which stipulates that the Rule of Law is not an arbitrary expression and exploitation of State power (Aristotle, 400BC).

In tragically ending the life of Jimmy Anderson by hanging, Tolbert and Oliver Bright precipitated their own savaged death 2 years later. Such tragedy and savagery of April 12, 1980 was followed by the execution of many Liberian officials on the beach 10 days later April 22. Moreover, the incivility of Doe and his "People Redemptive Council" in savagely killing AB Tolbert served as a major catalyst in obliterating Doe's reign of terror, which marked the continuation of Liberia's long dark night of her soul in culminating 10 years later in 1990 with the Lutheran Church Massacre of members of the Gio and Mano tribes by the government forces (AFL).

Why would a bunch of ignoramuses kill the basic enablers of intellectual bread in many interdisciplinary and innovative fields like Agriculture (J T Philips), Development Economics (D. Franklin Neal), Political Science and Diplomatic History (Cecil Dennis), Agricultural Economics and the Eisenhower Fellowship program in Marketing at Harvard (John Feweh Sherman), Political Science (Frank Tolbert), Banking and Finance (P Clarence Parker), Information and Culture, E. Reginald Townsend, a trailblazer in modern Journalism, whose innovation led to the formation of ELBC and ELTV, whose efforts furthered indigenous arts and culture, and their own Chief Justice of the Supreme Court James AA Pierre, a Bassa man? And Pierre, like the other 12 men had committed no crime. Instead, he facilitated the transformation of the Liberian Judiciary. As a graduate of Cuttington College and Divinity School in Maryland County, and one of the very best legal luminaries in the country, Justice Pierre placed Liberia on the world stage by participating with 5 other Chief justices at a mock trial known as the Belgrade Spaceship of the International Court of Justice in Belgrade, Yugoslavia. (Segal and Kriendler, 1972) The other justices were

Hidayatullah of India, Jovanovic of Yugoslavia, Burger of the US, Wold of Norway, and Crabble of Ghana. Additionally, he organized the West African Anglophone Chief Justices, which gave birth to ECOWAS Court of Justice to adjudicate regional disputes" (Segal and Kriendler, 1972).

Historically, there were others like Chief Justice Samuel Benedict who presided over the Constitutional Convention of 1847 and a signatory of the Declaration of Independence, Anthony William Gardiner, First Attorney General and signatory of the Declaration of Independence and later President who established the first Interior Department in his efforts of reaching out and integrating the settler and indigene classes, Senator A. Dash Wilson, an organic legal luminary during the period between Anthony William Gardiner's presidency and Alfred Francis Russell's 1 year term of office, who along with his wife Rachel Tubman were progenitors of Chief Justice A. Dash Wilson Jr., Chief Justice James Jenkins Dossen, former President of Liberia College and Vice President of the Republic, Chief Justice Louis Arthur Grimes, a hero of modern jurisprudence who as Secretary of State successfully defended his country at the League of Nations, thus, preventing British and French political conquest of Liberia, Clarence Lorenzo Simpson, Sr., an indigene, Montserrado County Attorney, Secretary of State, Head of the Liberian delegation to the League of Nations and who in service as Vice President was one of the organizers of the United Nations in 1945 and later served as Ambassador to the United States and the Court of St. James. Other legal luminaries included, Associate Justice O. Natty B. Davis who was unconstitutionally removed from the high court by Tubman. Despite his unjust removal, as a **Poor People's Lawyer**, O. Natty B's flamboyance and legal utterance were in consonance with the social justice of the Hebrew prophets, which found resonance with many Liberians. However, far from being perfect, President Tubman obviously included his repugnant action in his introspective confession to Almighty God for his "manifold sins and wickedness," a prayer that is found in the Protestant traditions. Here Nietzsche not only helps us in knowing Tubman's fear of losing power but also enables us in seeing how William Vacanarat Shadrach transcended such fear. Says Nietzsche, the transcendent man is:

> the pinnacle of self-overcoming, he rises above the human norm and above all difficulties, embracing whatever life throws at him. He is the one who overcomes mediocrity. He will be the happiest man, and as such, he is the meaning and justification of existence...Thus, to realize one's true self means not to envisage the self which lies deeply concealed within you, but rather the self that is immeasurably high over you.

There were also brilliant Justices like James N. Nagbe and John Africanus Dennis, Sr. who were forced to resign in 1987 by Samuel K. Doe, Justice Angie Brooks Randolph, First African President of the U.N. General Assembly and subsequently, the First Female Jurist of Liberia, Frances Johnson Morrison Allison, the First Female Chief Justice of Liberia who served for 1 year and later Attorney General in 2006, Gloria Musu Scott, Second Female Chief Justice who previously was Assistant Professor at the Louis Arthur Grimes School of Law, and Justice Jamesetta H. Wolokollie whose opinions and judicial activism on the high court speak for her tenacity and luminosity. Also, we have Chief Justice Henry Reed Cooper who served from 2003 – 2006. Justice Reed Cooper studied at the London school of Economics and the University of Pennsylvania Graduate School of Law.

As we ponder how does Liberia come out of her darkness, we turn to two of the country's great legal minds, Mohamedu Jones and Seward Cooper. Counselor Mohamedu F. Jones is a Summa Cum Laude graduate from the Louis Arthur Grimes School of Law and a Master of Law degree holder from Harvard University. As a legal scholar with a deep sense of humility and empathy for others, he continuously strives for the reconciliation of all Liberians. Seward Cooper is a graduate of the University of Liberia and the University of Wisconsin School of Law. In his brilliance, Seward Montgomery Cooper, Esq, called for reconciliation as he asked the nation via his *CWA Class of 70_50ᵗʰ Anniversary Speech* accordingly:

> What do we know about our country and our people? How did Liberia become a beacon of hope for the black race and a threat to colonialism and white racial domination? Why did we implode? Why do we still agitate in ways that could lead further to destruction? What can we do to uplift ourselves?

And like Martin Luther King, Jr, he cited from that illuminating thinker from Harvard, James Russell Lowell, In the strife of Truth with falsehood, for the good or evil side, Truth forever on the scaffold, wrong forever on the throne, Yet that scaffold sways the future, and behind the dim unknown, Stands God within the shadow keeping watch over his own. Despite some prayer by some of its sincere-loving citizens, Liberia in its regressive despair has continued to experience darkness permeating its horizons because of the absence of accountability and the pervasive presence of impunity. As we have asserted elsewhere in Murv L. Kandakai Gardiner's *Dostoevsky and Africa's Existential Abyss,* Liberia continues to sit on a very terrible abyss amidst the ritualistic killings because of impunity. And as Jean Calvin underscored in 16th century Geneva, "Nothing is more at variance with our faith than the foolish and irrational desires of ambitions" (1567). In the same article above-mentioned, we referenced Thomas Jefferson who said, "I tremble for my country when I reflect that God is just, and that his justice does not sleep forever" (Jefferson, 1781). If even Jefferson could go through introspection regarding America, then so must we amidst the moral degeneracy and pervasive presence of impunity in Liberia. In one of his best literary masterpieces, *The Possessed (Be'sy),* Dostoevsky says, "If you want to conquer the world, conquer yourself" (Dostoevsky, 1872). In *Be'sy* rampant murders were attributable to pervasive political and moral nihilism in mid-nineteen century Russia. Commensurately, according to Front Page Africa, "Gory killings in homes have become rampant in Monrovia" (Johnson, 2021). Like the nihilism which overflowed mid-nineteen century Russian society, the moral nihilism is overtaking twenty-first century Liberian society despite the existence of Christian and Islamic institutions. In Dostoevsky's magnus opus *Crime and Punishment,* Raskolnikov was preoccupied with rationalizing the moral basis of his deviant behavior without any clue to the psychological basis that includes his consciousness. Very deep in her darkness, Liberia has had criminals who were always delirious. And they sought to rationalize the psychopathic killings for the good of the people. Even Bai T. Moore has shown in his *Murder in the Cassava Patch* that evil cannot be rationalized. And the reality of indentured servitude and its consequential hardship cannot justify evil. The greatest American thinker and orator of the 18th century, Patrick Henry once said,

> Bad men cannot make good citizens. It is impossible that a nation of infidels or idolaters should be a nation of freemen. It is when people forget God that tyrants forge their chains. A vitiated state of morals, a corrupted public conscience, is incompatible with freedom. No free government, or the blessings of liberty, can be preserved to any people but by a firm adherence to justice.

A Liberian Senator who has been sanctioned by the U.S. Government for the very corrupt political practice of Pay-for-Play in selling the votes of many citizens of his home County, the man who on video argued that he was entitled to the presidency instead of Dr. Amos Sawyer or Charles Taylor as he rationalized, "I killed Doe, therefore, I should be president," along with other psychopathic criminals, plunged Liberia further in her darkness, which resulted in her stagnation and lifelessness.

At least Patrick Henry who became the First Governor of Virginia was conscious of his own darkness and the darkness of Britain and America. Harlow Unger in his *Lion of Liberty* discusses how Henry, in his darkness, came to terms with his inner dialectic. On the one hand, Henry was against slavery, which he strongly felt was a "lamentable evil" as he sought to abolish its importation to America. Yet on the other hand, he succinctly stated, "I cannot justify owning slaves, but I am not conflicted enough about actually setting anyone free" (Unger, 2010).

Again, how does Liberia extricate herself from this deep darkness? Do most Liberians understand their National Anthem? And did most Americans understand what Patrick Henry meant by "Give me liberty or give me death?" Henry was not speaking of just removing the shackles of physical bondage. He was talking about psychological and spiritual liberation in destroying the idols of oppression that were against God his maker. If it had not been for Patrick Henry and God by his side, there would be no American nation. And if there had been no American nation, there would be no Liberian nation. Do most Liberian officials who wear the mask of ethnicity know what the National Anthem is portraying as they sing, "This land of glorious liberty shall long be ours." What makes it glorious? Have hearts been united? Who benighted the black race, whites or Africans or both? Who according to Daniel Bashiel Warner, plunged the black race into intellectual and moral ignorance? Do most Liberians understand that in writing the National Anthem in 1847, Warner was situating the country's quest for Independence from the American Colonization Society on the freedom of the mind? And as a free born black man from Baltimore, Maryland, USA, like Patrick Henry, he may have understood that without God, psychologically they the pioneers of the nation would remain in fetters to tyranny and imperialism. This was the dynamic that Edward Wilmot Blyden asserted 34 years later after Liberia's Declaration of Independence that "If slavery finds residence in the mind, it becomes far more subversive than the ancient physical fetters" (Blyden, 1881).

And apparently, being a God-fearing man, Warner knew that without united hearts, without love for their indigenous sisters and brothers, there would be no true freedom for the young Liberian nation. Therefore, he actuated the first settler outreach in journeying into the depth culture (interior) of Liberia, which was led by Benjamin J.K. Anderson just 21 years later after Liberia's Independence in 1868. A major success of this undertaking was a covenantal relationship between Liberia and Mousadou, which unfortunately, later became part of Guinea due to French encroachment in the region. Did Warner anticipate that 176 years later, disunity among various indigenous tribes that is accompanied with strong hostility toward some "America-Liberian" political candidates would become an "Albatross "/psychological curse (S.T. Coleridge) in perpetuating severe human suffering in the country?

In Tolbert, Oliver Bright, Nelson Toe, Chea Cheapoo, Samuel Doe, Wessen, Prince Johnson, General Mosquito, Charles Taylor, and others, the voice of the God resounded like it did after Cain killed his brother Abel, "Cain where is your brother Abel?" (Genesis 4: 9a)" In cowardice and shame and even with weak defense mechanisms, like gordian worms crawling out of dead frogs, these men above mentioned, like Cain, answered in futile manipulation, "I don't know, Am I my brother's keeper?" The Lord said, "Your brother's blood cries out to me from the ground. Now you are under a curse and driven from the ground, which opened its mouth to receive your brother's blood from your hand…You will be a restless wanderer on the earth." (9b – 12)

6

The Prophetic and Political Feminism of Ruth Sando Fanbulleh Perry

Our astemarish (teacher) at Harvard Medical School of Continuing Studies, Carol Gilligan, in her in-depth seminar, *The Psychology of Love* taught us that feminism is asserting a voice, a different voice on behalf of the voiceless in the face of disconnection and injustice. For Professor Gilligan, true feminism has never been about bashing men. Instead, it has always sought the parity and equity of both genders and the preservation of this sacred earth. Like Sophocles' Antigone in Greek antiquity who courageously defied the unjust law of not being able to bury her brother Polyneices, out of love (***philos***) and courage (***andreia***), 21st century feminism questions the unjust laws of the land.

Henry David Thoreau gave impetus to the feminism of antiquity and the emerging feminism in modernity when he asserted in his *Civil Disobedience* that "people owe it to themselves and their fellow man not to blindly follow their government if they believe their rules and laws are unjust." Antigone sets the stage for Ruth Perry when she emphasizes that a greater law (*Themis*), a divine law, which depicts order and justice because of its foresight and prophecy impels her to bury the brother she loves. She

59

strongly feels that if it is a crime to bury her brother, then it is a crime that God demands. Also, in her *Women, Freedom, and Calvin,* Professor Jane Dempsey Douglas elucidates for us how Jean Calvin implicitly echoes the prophetic feminism of Antigone in Greek antiquity, as he emphasizes that "Women silence in the church has never been a matter of divine and eternal law that binds the conscience…instead, such terrible silence was predicated on human law relating to human governance, to the political life of the church" (Douglas, 1985). In *Antigone of The Oedipus Cycle,* Antigone goes on to say, "If I must die, I shall know the truth in death. *(aletheia sto thanatos)."* Antigone cannot forgo the truth about herself and the truth of God. Even in death she believes she shall know the truth like later Job, the wounded lover who could not forgo the truth. Like Antigone, propelled by the love of her husband and her people in Grand Cape Mount County and her country Liberia, Ruth Fanbulleh Perry became the embodiment of courage in actively campaigning for McDonald Perry, running for the Senate in 1985 and having the inner strength to work in the legislature in the face of tyranny in the executive branch of the government that was caused by paranoia and anxiety.

Also, like her antecedent and namesake in Hebraic antiquity, Ruth, daughter in law to Naomi, who moved from obscurity to prophetic identity when she said, "Please do not force me to stay away from you, I will go wherever you go, and I will stay wherever you stay, your people will be my people and your God my God (Ruth 1:16), Ruth Fanbulleh Perry said in 1985, "You cannot help by staying away." Thus, she accepted her seat in the Liberian Senate. Ruth Perry had the foresight and insight of prophecy. For according to Rabbi Abraham Heschel, prophecy is not simply prognostication, instead, it is insight into the desolation or pathos of God, which the prophet bears (Heschel, 1962).

The prophetic and political feminism of Ruth Perry not only paved the way for Ellen Johnson Sirleaf to become the 1st Elected President of Liberia and Africa as a whole, it transformed the political landscape in preparing other African nations to elect female presidents. The prophetic and political feminism of Ruth Perry also gave impetus to South African's Nkosazana Dlamini-Zuma who became the 3rd Chairperson of the African Union Commission. Mrs. Zuma asserted in May 2015 before President Obama in Addis Ababa, that there could have been no America without Africa, considering how African slaves built the U.S. Capitol, Constitutional Hall, the Executive Mansion (WH) and fertilized the U.S, economy with African slave labor. The prophetic and political feminism of Ruth Perry laid the foundations for Matsepe Cassaburi of South Africa (2005), Rose Francine Rogombe, Interim President of Gabon (June 2001 – October 2009), Agnes Monique Ohsan, Acting President of Mauritius (March – July 2012 and May – June 2015), Joyce Hilda Banda, President of Malawi (April 2012 – May 2014), Catherine Samba, Acting President of Central African Republic (January 2014 – March 2016), Sylie Kinigi, Acting President of Burundi (July 10, 1993 – February 7, 1994), Ameenah Gurib-Fakim, President of Mauritius (June 2015 – March 2018), and Sahle- Work Zewde, President of Ethiopia (October 2018 – Present).

The prophetic and political feminism of Ruth Perry is an echo of Tolstoy's prophetic and political feminism as he called attention in his masterpiece, *Resurrection*. Tolstoy's ***Anastasia (Resurrection)*** is essentially about love for the down-trodden, the voiceless, and for God's sacred earth.

We cannot overemphasize that what is highly elucidative in *Resurrection* is love. For with Tolstoy, love is the answer. Despite the unjust social stratification with its "moral bankruptcy and the inadequacy of the criminal justice system in St. Petersburg" (Tolstoy, 1899), the hope of Tolstoy's hero, Dmitri Nekhlyudov was anchored in his love for Katyusha Maslova, which magnified his love for God his creator. Interestingly, Dmitri means lover of the earth. Thus, Tolstoy's *Resurrection* is pivotally about the liberation and preservation of God's sacred earth.

Comparably, for Ruth Perry, love was/is the answer. Love enabled her to pioneer special outreach efforts like "Women Initiative in Liberia," "Women in Action for Goodwill," and "The Association of Special Services that sought to end the growing Liberian Civil War." Therefore, when the Economic Community of West African States (ECOWAS) effectively mediated a cease-fire in 1996 after 7 years of conflict, Ruth Perry out of love for country agreed to serve as Chairman of the Ruling Council, which made her Africa's 1st Female Head of State. However, regressive despair and the resignation of many Liberians occurred in the aftermath of the 1997 election that brought Charles Taylor to power. Such regressive despair and resignation were at variance with the will of God. As John Calvin puts it, "Since we are not our own, we must seek the glory of God" (Calvin, 1536). But Liberians did not seek the glory of God. They, as Calvin would put it, did not look up at the **Shamayim** (the mirror of the heavens) where God's palace shines with its brightness and auspiciousness in shaping our lives. For this reason, many Liberians found themselves dwelling in the necropolis/cemetery where in the words of Erich Fromm, they psychologically became "Zombies" as they chanted for Taylor, "You killed my ma, you killed my pa, but I'll vote for you." For these Liberian Zombies as Fromm suggests, their souls were dead while their bodies were alive. For Marx and Fromm, "money is the rule of the dead over the living…As alienation accelerates, society gets populated by the 'living dead' who ultimately destroys humanity and nature" (Thorpe, 2016). In Charles Taylor's reign of terror, we saw not only a repetitive cyclical death of Adam (man), we also witnessed the pervasive death of Adamah (the earth) through his raping of Liberia's forest and participating in blood diamonds that were precipitated by his greed and ignorance.

In her prophetic and political feminism Ruth Sando Fanbulleh Perry challenges us to be conscientious and assiduous toward our first love Adamah (Mother Earth/Mama Africa). Like Queen Esther of Susa who found herself amidst the sycophancy that was leading to the ultimate annihilation of her people, Ruth Perry faced similar challenge in Liberia. One cannot help wondering what was going on in the mind of Esther, an innocent Queen. On the surface only the obliteration of the ***imago dei,*** the eclipse of the divine, is apparent as the Jews seemed domed victims of a well-financed state genocide. Esther's inner world is clouded with fear. Her people, already marginalized, are about to be annihilated. As Queen of Persia, she has some ceremonial power. Yet as a woman and an alien, she is powerless. Esther prayed, "O God, save us from the hands of evildoers. And save me from my fear!" (The Apocrypha of the Book of Esther 14: 19) Andre LaCocque in *The Feminine Unconventional,* stresses the imposed need for women to espouse unusual causes. After her inner struggle and subsequent relief through prayer, Esther became courageous to think the unthinkable and do the impossible in breaking with the norms embedded within a Patriarchal society. In consequence and in spiritual resonance, she responded to Mordecai's prophecy on her being chosen by God for such a time as this, "gather all the Jews to be found in Susa. Hold a fast on my behalf and neither eat nor drink for three days, night or day. My maids and I will also fast as you do. Then I will go to the King even against the law: and if I perish, then I perish." (4:15 –16 16) Centuries later African American women of courage Fannie Lou Hamer, Sojourner Truth, Rosa Parks, Harriet Tubman, Shirley Chisholm, Sheila Jackson Lee, Maxine Waters, and Liberia's enablers of psychological and spiritual bread Ruth Fanbulleh Perry and Leymah Roberta Gbowee echoed Esther's words of faith and courage in pursuit of liberation, "If I perish, then I perish

7

Plato's Republic and the Hebraic and African Unconscious as they Pertain to Intellectual Bread

The Republic has long been the canon of Western intellectual development for various reasons. However, primarily, the centrality of *The Republic* itself is the unconscious/subconscious where some of the most significant events in Greek history and facets of political and cultural anxieties are understood. The subconscious is indeed that deep reservoir of thoughts, power, creative possibilities, and spiritual depository of our ancestors that even Zarathustra, the Hebrew prophets and psalmists, Edward Wilmot Blyden, Friedrich Nietzsche, Sigmund Freud, and Carl Jung have not taken for granted.

In this brief explication, I will simply reference Piraeus that port city, which signified not only economic strength but also intellectual and spiritual development. It was at Piraeus where Socrates descended as he himself was embarking upon the trajectory of transformation, *gnotti seauton* (know yourself). I will also look at the trios that impact the African unconscious, which we find in the Allegory of the Cave namely, *paideia* (efficacy of education), *aletheia* (reality/truth), and *elutheria* (freedom) as they pertain to Liberia. Here we can look at the nexus of Greek intellectual sophistication as it pertains to true liberation and the African unconscious/subconscious.

As soon as Socrates makes his descent into Piraeus, he tells us in Book 1 that justice is the soul of the State. With respect to Liberia, is injustice the heart of the soul of the State? Bearing in mind that like Piraeus, all major port cities including Carthage in antiquity, Tripoli, Mombasa, Lagos, and Monrovia in modernity were all port cities that pivotally shaped the destiny of the soul of their respective State. Since its inception, the Free Port of Monrovia has been very significant in facilitating the imports of technology, finished goods of rubber, varieties of materials for building and construction, and educational and medical supplies for the government and various church organizations. On the flip side, the Free Port of Monrovia has historically been monumental in shipping large quantities of rubber and iron ore for steel production to America and Europe. Amidst all of this, we ask, what is the soul of Liberia, and where is it? Unequivocally, the soul of Liberia is injustice. Aristotle in antiquity asserted that the Rule of Law was established to shape governance. In his *Politics 3.10* he averred, "Where the vision of freedom reigns, the rule of law is not an arbitrary expression of state power but is shaped around the ideal that we may live as we wish so long as we do not transgress against the person or property of another" (Aristotle, 400 BC). As part of the African unconscious, can the soul of Liberia be redirected for the true redemption of the Liberian people?

Here we are impelled to look at the terrible corrupt practices of some of our past and current government officials for not challenging the disingenuous policies of Firestone and ArcelorMittal Corporations.

Liberia is a culture of fear. Yet this culture finds itself in the presence of empathic resonance amidst the physical and psychological brutality caused by obsequious sycophancy.

Still part of the larger question remains, is the soul of Liberia buried with large deposits of Iron Ore in Mount Gangra, Nimba, Bong Mines, and the Putu Mines of Grand Gedeh and Gold deposits in Grand Kru Counties? Or as it awaits its resurrection from external and internal degradation, will the soul of Liberia come to fruition in experiencing justice as Socrates and the Hebraic-prophetic pragmatists in antiquity accentuated? Like *The Republic* and Hebraic sub/unconscious, the African unconscious claims justice as its very soul.

In Hebraic tradition, mishpatim is the word employed for jurisprudence or laws governing interpersonal, behavioral relationships appertaining to money, lending, crime, punishment, and other facets of exchangeability of goods and services. But Tsedakah (Greek dikaiosune and Arabic Al'sadaq) means that justice is intertwined with righteousness with heavy focus on compassion. Justice highlights the ethical and charitable dimensions of life (Halevi and Nachmanides). Here with economic justice, a philanthropist enables one to become self-sufficient by assisting him or her with a loan or gift to start an initiative /business. And this is the highest level of charity (Maimonides). Begging is seriously discouraged. God himself calls for justice to roll down like waters and righteousness like an overflowing stream. (Amos 5: 24)

Book 1 in the beginning of *The Republic* describes justice as forward moving, which begins as a downward trajectory of the soul as Socrates posits, "I went down into the Piraeus" before embarking upon its upward trajectory. And just before his public execution in drinking the hemlock, Socrates asserted, "The unexamined life is one not worth living, for unrighteousness runs deeper that death." We are challenged by Sen Armah Jallah to see the pervasive injustices in Liberia like the unconstitutional impeachment of Justice Kabineh Ja'neh. And Ibn Khaldun still confronts us that "the social function of law and justice is to ensure a stable social order" (Khaldun, 1377). In view of the above, Liberians are called to resist the forces of cacodaemon (evil spirits). By choosing the eudaemon (inner voice of goodness) as Socrates did, that is the only way we can sustain and further the justice for which Socrates, Jesus, and the Prophets of Israel, and the Nabi (Prophet) Mohammed died. Meshach Neufville has been very insightful in averring that many Liberians have defiled the eudaemon. And because many of them have contaminated the eudaemon, it is difficult to unfetter them from the caves of shadows.

In Book VII Socrates teaches us as he elucidates how *paideia* (education) begins the journey toward *elutheria* (freedom) from the cave when it enters the anthropini psuche (human soul) not to remain dormant, but to stir the soul toward perceiving, intuiting, and framing a different *aletheia* (reality), a life beyond the cave of shadows when at last the eyes of former prisoners can look up at the heavens and see the sun as light. *Paideia*, which entails all facets of the arts and sciences (especially music), technology, and agriculture awaits Liberians in order to pass them through a new reality into psychological liberation.

Whether it is a modified theocracy or a stratified democracy, a man or woman who has been a warrior shall never be fit to lead God's people. Even King David came to terms with his wretchedness and unworthiness to the extent that because he had shed blood upon the earth in the sight of God, he was unfit to build the temple that would signify the presence of the holiness of God. (1 Chronicles 22: 8) And Jean Calvin in 16th century Geneva asserted that he or she who does not despise this world is not fit to participate in God's coming basileia (kingdom) with its redemptive justice in the world to come. This simply means that we should never be satisfied with the world as it is. It does not mean that violence is the solution to our problems. Change can come through faith, hope, and charity. Thus, we hereby call for the ICC to become operational in Liberia. Without justice what remains is the soul of Liberia being in mortal danger.

Bole Medhanealem

8

Bole Medhanealem: An Enabler of Spiritual and Intellectual Bread as a House of Prayer in its Totality

In this final chapter we look at spiritual and intellectual bread in one of the most beautiful houses of prayer in Africa. Bole Medhanealem is that beautiful house of prayer. Prayer becomes the means and end of spiritual and intellectual feeding. Here at Bole Medhanealem, people gathered even outside the gates of the Church like the ancients did at the Temple on Mount Moriah in Jerusalem in feeding their hungry souls by praying.

As the 2nd largest cathedral in Africa next to the Basilica of our Lady of Peace in Cote d'Ivoire, Bole Medhanealem at Bole, Addis Abba is a distinctive house of prayer as anticipated by Deutero-Isaiah and accentuated by Jesus. As I perambulated the verdant lawns and courtyard of this beautiful church, I was impressed with the deep sense of spiritual enrichment that many Ethiopians seek daily. I can never forget how fervently many Ethiopians stand or knell in prayer at various angles of the church. Unlike some other parts of Africa where several children are seen in the streets engaging in delinquency including prostitution, at Bole

Medhanealem, it is very common to find little girls and boys kneeling before the Cross (Meskel) in prayer.

Every time I see little boys and girls genuflecting at Bole Medhanealem in preparation for prayer, I realize that even now, Ethiopia stretches her hands up to God on behalf of a broken and shattered humanity (Psalm 68: 31). Ethiopian stretching forth her hands to God also became a pivotal tenet of the corporate spirituality of the Ethiopian Orthodox Tewahedo Church in resisting Italian occupation and obliterating all semblances of colonial conquest.

Jesus encountered corruption at the Jerusalem Temple. For him, it was the worst kind of corruption because the people had profaned the holiness (kidus/kadoshah) of God, by turning his house of worship into a market. With immediacy, he invoked two suffering servants, 2nd Isaiah and Jeremiah by saying, "My house shall be called a house of prayer" (Isaiah), but you have turned it into a den of thieves" (Jeremiah). He then proceeded to purify the temple by overturning the tables of the marketers and money changers. His stance was intricately linked with his concentration on healing (curing) the blind and lame right in the Temple. Thus, the blind and lame who were cured were witnesses to the power of God and true purpose of the Temple as the house where salvation holistically is mediated.

Thus, in view of Jesus' paradigm in antiquity, in modernity, we cannot confront and condemn corruption without appropriating and actualizing some compassion through anointing, healing, and almsgiving. We cannot engage in the rhetoric of corruption while we are quick to abuse other Liberians with British and American accents by raising the prices of food and other items in the market. Liberians ultimately rob themselves when they drain, deceive, and destroy the very people who are trying to help them. As a true house of prayer, Bole Medhanealem replicates God's holy Temple in the spiritual Jerusalem that was envisaged within Judaism and Christianity in antiquity. At Bole Medhanealem, one experiences not only the praises of Israel, but comes to appreciate how God (Egziabeher) also inhabits the praises of Ethiopia in his holy Temple.

In celebrating the birth of our Savior during Christmas midnight service January 7, 2012, I found the liturgical experience at the Cathedral to be very uplifting. The Ethiopian Orthodox Tewahedo Church enables a very deep spiritual presence via its trajectory of inner/deeper sanctuary in commensurate with the Aaronic Priestly Order in ancient Israel. Its chants and melodies were influenced by 6th century Christianity from the Kingdom of Axum, especially, the compositions of the distinctive Orthodox personage, Saint Yared. But the highest point of my creative pilgrimage is the celebration of Transfiguration, which is commonly known as Buhe in August. At Buhe, traditional singers and dancers personify Mounts Tabor and Hermon in illustrating God's holy Mountains anticipating the crucifixion of Jesus and his resurrection (Tinsia) on the 3rd day.

In my sojourn on this earth, I am thankful to God to have residences in Liberia and America. But my ancestral presence is ultimately felt in Ethiopia as I hear echoes of my mother's and grandmother's prayers over here, as I experience the sensation of roasted coffee (buna) everywhere, and as I listen to liturgical, classical, and jazz music that remind me of my father Theodore and brother Tilmon. Just before his sudden death in August 2012, the late Abune Paulos (His Holiness) of the Ethiopian Orthodox Tewahedo Church, my astamari (teacher), spiritual elder brother and friend since our days of studies in the States at Princeton, wanted me to labor with him at Axum, Tigray in appropriating my skills in Keynesian economics and developmental psychology in service to Christ. As a depth psychologist with an anthropological and ecological focus, obviously, I sustained a heavy loss personally because of his death.

My dad Theodore (Theodoros/God-given) endowed me with this prayer, which was a special gift from his dad Theophilus (loving God). Out of the depths I cry to you, O Lord. Lord, hear my voice. Let your ears be attentive to the voice of my supplication…I wait for the Lord. My soul does wait. And in his word do I hope. Unlike Job 19, which is derivative culturally from the experience of a wounded lover within a male/female relationship and later appropriated to the sufferer (Job) and his Creator in the I/Thou relationship, Psalm 130 is a song of songs. It was in the abyss itself that this psalmist cried to his God beneath the floods. If ever there was only one life-saving psalm, it is this one. Later it was extrapolated by many Ethiopians in Hebrew who were coming out of the depths of destruction in 1980. And this love song is very life-affirming. For Falashas Jews whom the Israeli government rescued, their song became known as Mima'akim (Out from the Depths).

> From deep depths I called to you to come to me
> With your return the light in my eyes will come back.
> Who is it that calls to you tonight?
> Who will give his life, put it underneath you?
> Who will be like dust living at your feet?
> Who will love you of all your lovers,
> Who will save you from all evil spirits from the deep depths?

As one of my favorite German scholars once averred, "We are separated from the mystery, the depth, the origin, and greatness of our existence. We hear the voice of that depth, but our ears are closed. We try to escape the urgency of it and will not accept its promise" (Tillich, 1955). Bole Medhanealem means Savior and medicine for the world. It was not in his superiority to suffering but rather in his serenity amidst the suffering that Jesus was able to make healing efficacious on the Cross. In our study here, we see a historical irony because Flavius Josephus asserted that it was Saba, Queen of Sheba who first took the balm to Old Jerusalem in Palestine when she visited King Solomon way before the special healing medicine was associated with Gilead in Trans Jordan. Yet despite Saba's historical visit to Jerusalem and the apparent medically anthropological breakthrough with the balm (medicine), 6th century Ethiopian Christians situated the focus and locus of healing on the Man of Sorrows, the one who hung on the Cross for them, the one whose very look at them with outstretched arms saves them. In enabling spiritual and intellectual bread to its people by corporately praying daily and fervently, Ethiopia is also prospering economically, technologically, and socio-culturally because righteousness exalts a nation (Proverbs 14:34).

We began this body of critical thought with Africa our native land with bread in its starving land. Now we bring it to a close with Africa our mother as projected by one of the greatest Ethiopian artists, Teddy Afro who happens to also be an Ethiopian Orthodox Tewehado Christian. Beginning the song, *Adey,* Africa my mother my life with the flute, Teddy enables everyone to experience the inner harmony of his/her soul with the soul of Ethiopia. In listening to the flute playing in *Adey,* one can feel the sound of the land itself and how Africa as **Ayana** blossoms eternally. **Adey** begins accordingly,

> be'Africa semayi siri.
> Enate setwelgigne gena aynishin say
> Bemayleka fikir,
> Under the sky of Africa
> When I see your eyes after
> You gave birth to me
> You love me unconditionally…
> Ayemaye ayemaye (my mother, my mother in Amharic)
> Adey Adey – (mom, mom in Tigrinian)

My homeland mama Ethiopia. Teddy's love for Africa is deepened in the song, *Adey*. Ironically, *Adey* also means mother in Grebo. Thank God for Ethiopia and for enabling Bread in a starving Africa.

Conclusion

In my explication of the historiae of Liberia, the Episcopal Church of Liberia, the Gardiner Family, and the Civilizational Excellency of Ethiopia, I passionately sought to drive home the point that there has always been bread in Liberia a Starving Africa. But darkness, suffering, and regressive despair have kept many Liberians from seeing Jesus the Eternal Loaf who is the totality of human existence. It is our hope that through prayer, which is an act of surrender and spiritual feeding and digesting, many eyes shall be opened. No matter how difficult or impossible a situation might be, Jesus the *Eternal Bread* from Heaven challenges us to think the unthinkable and do the impossible as He sustains us daily. As we seek the **Bread** daily, let us be mindful that we can never see Jesus without be challenged to change our mindset, our sense of values, and commitment to serve and transform the world. And as we have increasingly accentuated, love is bread because it feeds our minds, our souls, and keeps us connected with God our maker, His people and His sacred earth.

Despite cultural divergence and ethnocentrism at the inception of Liberia as a Republic, there were trailblazers of true liberation who were sincere about reconciliation and integration of the indigenes and settlers groups such as King Sao Boso Kamara, J.J. Roberts, Daniel B Warner,

Clarence L. Simpson, Sr., and Louis Arthur Grimes. As adolescents traveling back to Africa, perhaps the pioneers of a new country were subconsciously affected by the voice of the Water of the Atlantic Ocean, which were echoes of their African foremothers and forefathers crying out to them, in prompting them to obliterate all forms of slavery. Such cry could not be erased from their soul, "O water voice of my heart, crying in the sand, is it the voice of my heart or the voice of the sea, is it I, is it I? All night long the water is crying to me" (Symons).

To authentically address the poverty and misery of the suffering masses, Liberians should refrain from cussing and disrespecting their president. A protest rally with the aim of alleviating the suffering in Liberia should emulate the 1963 March on Washington through which Martin Luther King, Jr. dawned upon the conscience of an American nation in calling for the US to be true to its fundamental principles. For this reason, while we applaud Alexander Cummings' initiatives in education, he should not have allowed Lewis Brown and others to exclude other opposition political parties and disrespect the President and the Ruling Party. In the spirit of Reconciliation, members of all political parties should have been invited to cooperatively address the plight of the nation. "If you sincerely want to overcome the world with all of its challenges, first learn how to overcome yourself," as Dostoevsky reminds us from his pen.

Just as *Padeia* (enlightened education as intellectual bread) awaits Liberians in order to remove them from the "caves of shadows" (Plato), and take them to the point where they can look up and see the truth and light (*aletheia),* and at last be free, Jesus the ***Eternal Bread*** from Heaven awaits Liberians to seek him in order that He may feed their hungry souls spiritually and intellectually. It is our hope that not only Liberians but all Africans and the entire global village will seek this intellectual and spiritual bread and be feed daily. For in the midst of helplessness and hopelessness, there is another option, ***Eternal Bread.***

References

a'Kempis, Thomas. (1427 & 1643). *The Imitation of Christ.* Cologne, Germany Joannis Kinckii Publisher

Archives of the Episcopal Church. (2012). "The Rev Alexander Crummell 1819-1898." *The Church Awakens: African Americans and the Struggle for Justice.* New York

Anderson, Gerald. (1998). *Biographical Dictionary of Christian Missions.* Grand Rapids, Michigan: W. B. Eerdmans Publishing Company

Aristotle. (350 BCE). *Politics 3:10,* Athens, Greece

Augustine, St. (426 A.D.). *The City of God against the Pagans.* Carthage, 2nd Publication, Cambridge University Press

Baker, Henry Williams. (1868). *The King of Love My Shepherd Is.* Ireland and Wales, United Kingdom

Barclay, Edwin J. (1909). *The Lone Star Forever.* Monrovia, Liberia

Blyden, Edward Wilmot. (1887). *Christianity, Islam, and the Negro Race.* London, England: W.B. Whittingham & Company

_____, _____. (1873). *From West Africa to Palestine.* Manchester & London: John Haywood; Simpkin Marshall & Co

Boff, L. (1983). *The Lord's Prayer: The Prayer of Integral Liberation*: Maryknoll: Orbis

Bousma, William. (1989). *John Calvin: A Sixteen Century Portrait.* Oxford, England: Oxford University Press

Calvin, John. (1536). *Institutes of the Christian Religion.* Basel, Switzerland.

Calvin, John. (1557). *Calvin's Commentary on the Psalms, Part V: Psalm 127.* Vol 12 Christian Classics Ethereal Library

_____, _____. (1555). *Harmony of the Evangelists: Matthew, Mark, and Luke.* Edinburgh, Scotland: Trans by the Rev Pringle

_____. _____. (1955). *Institutes of the Christian Religion.* Trans by John Allen, Presbyterian Board of Christian Education. Bk III, Chapter IX,1 New York

_____. _____. (1986). *Institutes of the Christian Religion* (1536 ed) Trans and edited by Ford Lewis Battles. Grand Rapids: Wm. B. Eerdmans Publishers

Caputu, John D. (1997). *Deconstruction in a Nutshell: A Conversation with Derrida.* New York, NY: Fordham University Press

Charcot, Jean-Martin. (1888). *Lecons sur les maladies du systeme nerveux.* Lectures on the Diseases of the Nervous System. Paris, France

Coker, Daniel. (1820). *Prayer at Sea* recorded in James Washington's *Conversation with God.* New York, NY: HarperCollins Publishers

Cone, James. (1975). *God of the Oppressed.* New York, NY: Seabury Press

Cooper, Seward Montgomery. (1996). *The Coopers of Liberia: A Brief Genealogy.* Reston, Virginia

Cramer, Thomas. (1547). *The 1928 Book of Common Prayer.* Great Britain, UK

Crummell, Alexander. (1862). *The Future of Africa: Addresses, Sermons Delivered In the Republic of Liberia.* New York, NY: Charles Scribner

Derrida, Jacques. (1967). *Deconstruction.* Paris, Francis: Gayatri Chakravorty Spivak

Douglas, Jane Dempsey. (1985). *Women, Freedom, and Calvin.* Louisville, KY: Westminster John Knox Press

Dubois, W.E.B. (1903). "On the Rev Alexander Crummell" in *The Souls of Black Folk.* Chicago, IL: A.C. McClurg and Company

Dunn, Elwood. (1992). *A History of the Episcopal Church of Liberia, 1821 – 1980.* Metuchen, NJ, and London: American Theological Library Association and The Scarecrow Press

Eliot, T.S. (1942). "For us, there is only trying" in *Four Quartets.* London, England: Faber and Faber Publisher

Erikson, Erik H. (1981). *The Galilean Sayings and the Sense of the "I".* New Haven, CT: Yale Review Vol 70, 321-362

_____, _____. (1963). *Stages of Psychosocial Development.* New York: W.W. Norton and Company

_____, _____. (1966). *Human Strength and the Cycle of Generations.* New York: W.W. Norton and Company

_____, _____. (1963). *Childhood and Society.* New York: W.W. Norton & Company

Fanon, Frantz. (1959). *A Dying Colonialism.* Paris, France: Francois Maspero Publisher

_____, _____. (1961). *The Wretched of the Earth.* France: Francois Maspero Publisher

Frank, Anne. (1947). *Anne Frank: The Diary of a Young Girl.* The Netherlands: Contact Publishing Company

Freud, Sigmund. (1930). *Civilization and its Discontent.* Vienna, Austria: Internationaler

Psychoanalytischer Verlag Wlen Publisher

Fromm, Erich. (1970). *Psychoanalysis and Religion.* New Haven: Yale University Press

Gardiner, Murv L. (2001). *Predestination and Liberation: Some Often Overlooked Influences from the Text of John Calvin and Some Obvious and Hidden Meaning* of Calvinism. Ann Arbor, Michigan: UMI Publisher & Library of Congress

Gardiner, Murv L. Kandakai. (2017). *Edward Wilmot Blyden's Contribution to Intellectual History: Transcending Gender, Race, and Ethnicity.* Atlanta, GA: The Perspective Magazine. Also reprinted in the Liberian Studies Journal (2017) (2020) Vol 42, Durham, NC: Published by Liberian Studies Association, INC

Gardiner, Murv L. Kandakai_____. (2021). *Dostoevsky and Africa'sExistential Abyss.* Atlanta, GA:The Perspective Magazine

Gutierrez, Gustavo. (1991). *The God of Life.* Maryknoll, New York: Orbits Books

Heber, Reginald. (1827). *Bread of the World in Mercy Broken.* Hodnet and Oxford, UK

Hegel, Georg F. (1807). *Phenomenology of Mind.* Heidelberg and Berlin, Germany: Bamberg and Worzberg Publisher

Heilbroner, Robert. (1975). *An Inquiry into the Human Prospect.* New York, NY: W.W. Norton and Company

Heschel, Abraham Joshua. (1955). *The Prophets.* Vol 1 New York: Harper & Row

_____. _____. (1962). *The Prophets.* New York: Harper Collins

Jensen, Jane S. (2008). *Women Political Leaders: breaking the highest glass ceiling.* New York, NY: Palgrave Macmillan

Jung, Carl G. (1933). *Modern Man in Search of a Soul.* London, England: Paul Kegan, Trubner Trench and Company

Kaufman, Peter Iver. (1990). *Redeeming Politics.* Princeton: Princeton University Press

Keynes, John Maynard. (1936). *The General Theory of Employment, Interest and Money.* London, UK: Macmillan Publisher

Khaldun, Ibn. (1377 & 1958). *The Muqaddimah.* Cairo, Egypt and Cambridge, England Cambridge University Press

Kieh, George. (2017). Referred to indigenous Liberians who find themselves in low socio-political sitz-im-leben as subaltern in his article *The Janus-Faced Liberian State* in The Liberian Studies Journal Vol 42, 2017 (2020) Durham, NC: Published by The Liberian Studies Association, INC.

LaCocque, Andre'. (1990). *The Feminine Unconventional.* Minneapolis: Augsburg Press

Luther, Martin. (1538). "Preface to Georg Rhau's Symphoniae icundae," in *Luther's Works,* Vol 53, pp. 321 – 322. Wittenberg, Germany

Lyte, Henry Francis. (1847). *Abide with Me Fast Falls the Evening Tide.* Scotland, United Kingdom: Published Posthumously 1850

Maimonides, Moses. (1180). *The Mishneh Torah.* Egypt

_____, _____. (1204). *Economic Justice and Jewish Values on Truth of the Holy Law.* Egypt

Maslow, Abraham. (1943). "Hierarchy of Needs: A Theory of Human Motivation" in the *Journal of Psychological Review.* Princeton and New York: American Psychological Association

_____, _____. (1962). *Toward a Psychology of Being.* Princeton, NJ: Van Nostrand Publisher

Moltmann, Jurgen. (1979). *The Future of Creation.* Minneapolis, Minnesota: Augsburg Fortress Publisher

Matteo, Thomas. (2011). *The World Leaders Who Walked Among Us.* New York. Staten Island Advance

New York Times. (1941). *T. M. Gardiner 71 Bishop of Liberia Dies.* New York, NY: April 1941

New York Times. (1996). *New Interim Leader is Chosen for Liberia.* New York, NY: Retrieved January 10, 2017

Niebuhr, Reinhold. (1932). *Moral Man and Immoral Society.* New York, NY: Charles Scribner's and Sons

Nietzsche, Friedrich. (1886). *The Birth of Tragedy.* Leipzig, Germany: E.W. Fritzsch Publisher

_____, _____. (1878). *Human All Too Human.* Trans by Alexander Harvey, Leipzig, Germany: Ernst Schmeitzner Publisher

_____, _____. (1883) *Thus Spoke Zarathustra.* Leipzig, Germany: Ernst Schmeitzner Publisher

_____, _____. (1895). *The Antichrist.* Trans by H.L. Mencken, Leipzig, Germany: Oscar Levy Publisher Plato. (399 BC). *Apologia Socratis.* Athens, Greece.

_____. (375 BC). *The Republic.* Ancient Greece.

Rauschenbusch, Walter. (1960). *Christianity and the Social Crisis.* New York, NY: The MacMillan Company

Robinson, Marilynne. (1998). *The Death of Adam.* New York: Houghton Mifflin

Rogers, Carl. (1951). *Client-centered Therapy: Its Current Practices, Implications and Theory*. Boston: Houghton Mifflin Publisher

Reuther, Rosemary R. (1998). *Women and Redemption*. Minneapolis, MN: Fortress Press

Sachs, Jeffrey. (2005). *The End of Poverty: Economic Possibilities of our Time*. New York and London, England: Penguin Press

Samuelson, Paul. (1983). *Economics from the Heart*. San Diego: Harcourt Brace Jovanovich

Schopenhauer, Arthur. (1818). *The World as Will and Representation*. Dresden and Leipzig, Germany: Brodhaus Publisher and later Cambridge Univ Press

Schumacher, Ernst Friedrich. (1973). *Small is Beautiful: A Study of Economics As If People Mattered*. London, England: Blond and Briggs Ltd H

Schumpeter, Joseph. (1942). "Creative Destruction" in his *Capitalism, Socialism, and Democracy*. London, UK: Rutledge Press

Segal, Bernard G & Kriendler Louis. (1972). *The Belgrade Space* "trial". Cleveland, Ohio: World Peace Through Law Center

Sirleaf, Ellen Johnson. (2009). *This Child Will be Great*. New York: HarperCollins

Skard, Torild. (2014). "Ruth Perry" in *Women of Power Half a Century of female Presidents and prime ministers worldwide*. Bristol: Policy Press

Smith, Adam. (1776). "Invisible Hand" in *An Inquiry into the Nature and Causes of the Wealth of Nations*. London: W. Strahn and T. Cadell

Sophocles. (1958). *The Oedipus Cycle.* Trans by Dudley and Fritzgerald New York, NY: W.W. Norton & Company

Taylor, Jeremy. (1650). "Contentedness in Hard Circumstances" in his *Holy Living and Dying.* Golden Grove, England: Richard Vaughan Publishing Company

Thorpe, Charles. (2016). *Necroculture.* New York: Palgrave Macmillan

Tibebu, Tashalle. (2012). *The Counter Civilizing Mission: The Pan-Negrist Imagination of Africa in the 19th century West Coast of Africa.* Lawrenceville, New Jersey: Africa World Press and the Red Sea Press

Tillich, Paul. (1955). *The Shaking of the Foundations.* New York, NY: Charles Scribner's Sons

Tolstoy, Leo. (1899). *Resurrection.* St. Petersburg, Russia: Niva Publisher

Unger, Harlow Giles. (2010). *Lion of Liberty: Patrick Henry and the Call to a New Nation.* Boston, Massachusetts: Da Capo Press

Veblein, Thorstein. (1899). "Conspicuous Consumption" in *The Theory of the Leisure Class: An Economic Study of Institutions.* New York: MacMillan Company

Weatherhead, Leslie Dixon. (1981). *The Autobiography of Jesus: What Jesus Said about Himself.* London, UK: Festival Books Publisher

_____. _____. (1951 & 1975). *Psychology, Religion, and Healing.* London, UK and Nashville, TN: Hodder & Stroughton and Abingdon Cokesbury Press

Winter, Gibson. (1981). *Liberating Creation: Foundations of Religious Social Ethics.* New York: Crossroad Publishing Company

Printed in the United States
by Baker & Taylor Publisher Services